GEOGRAPHY

IN HUMAN DESTINY

Geography
In Human Destiny

By RODERICK PEATTIE, Ph.D.

ORIGINAL MAPS AND CHARTS DRAWN BY ARTHUR H. ROBINSON

GEORGE W. STEWART · PUBLISHER

NEW YORK CITY

GEORGE W. STEWART • PUBLISHER

Manufactured in the U.S.A. by VAN REES PRESS, *New York*

P.J.

To MARGARET *and* JOSEPH

PLATT

in return for criticism, beer

and Gemütlichkeit

Contents

Illustrations

Acknowledgements

I am grateful to Harcourt, Brace and Company for permission to quote from Virginia Woolf's "Orlando," and from J. Russell Smith's "North America," first edition; to Harper and Brothers to quote from Louis Adamic's "The Native's Return"; to Appleton-Century Company and George Hubbard to quote from his "Geography of Europe"; to J. B. Priestly and Harper & Brothers to quote from "English Journey"; to Houghton Mifflin & Co. and Willa S. Cather to quote from "My Antonia"; to Simon & Schuster and my brother D. C. Peattie to quote from "Green Laurels"; to Henry Holt & Co. and E. C. Semple to quote from "Influences of Geographic Environment." These quotations are noted in the text of this book. I am grateful also for permission to use the following illustrations: Figures 19 and 20 from Ellsworth Huntington's "Civilization and Climate," published by Yale University Press; and figures 24 and 25 from D. W. Johnson's "Topography and Strategy in the World War," published by Henry Holt and Company.

GEOGRAPHY

IN HUMAN DESTINY

Chapter One

ABOUT

THIS GEOGRAPHY

Not twenty years ago i was tramping the north shore of the Lower St. Lawrence Valley. This is the portion from Quebec to Labrador, a region where forests spill over the cliffs down to the water's edge, a region of clearings in the forests and, in those days, of inadequate roads. Indeed, the French Canadian *habitant* * living there used the canoe for so many years that when he did take to nag travel his phrase was (to translate), "I disembarked from my horse and moored

* *Habitant* is a delightful French Canadian word defining the inhabitant of the land who has essentially a peasant psychology.

it to a tree." I had in my wanderings come to Tadoussac. This settlement, born as a fur-trading station, is at the mouth of the Saguenay River which for ninety miles lies along a cleft in the uplands, a great fiord. The houses of Tadoussac stand on a rocky point at the confluence of the two rivers. Beleaguered there by rain, as the phrase goes, I fell in with an anthropologist. Now it is established that the less the density of population the greater the concentration of anthropologists—therefore the occasion calls for no surprise. It was due to the anthropologist that I had the following adventure.

We went to a log cabin that stood apart from the settlement. It was a rare bit of Americana. There were shutters at the windows reminiscent of the days of the bow and arrow. Over the door was carved H. B. C. which stood for Hudson Bay Company. The company has been so long established there that when I asked the meaning of the initials the quick reply was "Here Before Christ." Inside the cabin was one low-ceilinged room. The rafters were darkened by the past use of pine-knot torches. At one end there were some sleeping-alcoves. But attention was centered on the fire in a huge fireplace that literally made up one wall of the room. Beside the hearth was a young woman nursing a baby at the breast. Note the babe; he is an important part of my thesis. For the moment, an old man, the child's grandfather, held the stage, and a black-robed priest, with obvious delight, was listening to the man sing. The man was a *conteur,* one who knew the folk tales and folk songs. All afternoon we heard them, stories of the Round Table, the familiar Wagnerian legends, the pagan fairy tales. They were in French, of course, but in the patois of Normandy and Picardy of the days of Louis XIV, sung word for word as the *conteur's* father's father's father had sung them. The Middle Ages preserved into modern times.

Today, in the Lower St. Lawrence country there exists with official recognition the feudal system— *Mirabile dictu*—and this on American soil. Today, with a collective mind little disturbed by modernity, these French Canadians are Roman Catholics characterized by that purity of devotion which we think of as ending with the Middle Ages. There is in their common speech much that is sixteenth-century Norman. They use words obsolete, or with meanings obsolete, in modern France. Indeed, they still use the old Norman two-wheeled cart, harvest with a scythe, and thresh with a flail.

Let me return to the particular, to the babe in the mother's arms. Without the introduction of newspapers, movies and the radio forcing a chaos of modern ideas into the mind of the *habitant,* that suckling infant, now a man, has inherited from his grandfather the old tales. He knows and sings the same themes and sings them with the same ancient verbage and inflection. Unless modern confusion has forced the details from his mind you may visit him, or other *conteurs,* to hear the songs reproduced as I heard them that rainy afternoon at Tadoussac.

We know these retentions of old habits as crystallizations. Such crystallizations of past culture are direct response to the extent to which a people have lived apart. In other words, the preservation is a measure of the extent to which modern ideas have been excluded from the region. The *habitant* settlements have been so fortified by the forest barrier, and by the river dangerous to navigation for more than half of the year, that when the English took over Canada they felt that they could not force their culture upon these remote people. The *habitant* was left with right to fly the French flag, to use his own native tongue and later to have the *Code Napoléon* for his civil law. The upheaval of the French revolution did not touch these people. With difficulty were they aroused to enter the World War in defense of either France or England.

Such preservation of old ways of living is not uncommon. Though good roads and automobiles now have brought our own Appalachian mountain folk up-to-date, these people still sing from books of old musical notation and use language with Shakespearean form. A generation ago one mountain man was discovered hunting rabbits with an old English cross bow. At the end of the nineteenth century they were rightly called our contemporary ancestors. Some forms of Norse law still exist upon the Isle of Man which lies in the Irish Sea hardly out of sight of England. The Basques in northern Spain are said on occasion to practice the ancient *couvade,* the custom of the man's simulating the pangs of childbirth during his wife's confinement. These customs are anthropology or sociology, but their preservation is the matter of provincialism which so intrigues us. The search for oddity and quaintness helps fill our travel bureaus each spring. The truth is, that insofar as provincial contrasts can be explained by earth variations, that is by the physical makeup of the provincial regions, these contrasts are geography.

Let me hasten as a geographer to disown a scientific interest in many cultural habits. A great deal has been labeled geography which is not geography. We must distinguish between significant cultural features and mere cultural oddities. Too many people look upon any cultural peculiarity as geographic. One travel magazine, because the word "geographic" is used in its title, has done much to foster this misconception. Largely a picture magazine, its pages are too frequently of little geographic importance, with views of Japanese cherry blossoms beside the Potomac, or the statue of some local deliverer erected in a city plaza and surrounded by salvia plants. (*Why* do people plant salvia at the feet of all deliverers?)

It is not surprising that there is so much misunderstanding as to the purposes and content of geography. Our early geography consisted of location, location of anything. Under such concepts, in the first grade in a little white school house, I learned the counties of

Michigan. My father was called upon to chant the names of the capitals of the states together with the streams which served to carry away their sewage. The chant began, of course, with "Augusta-on-the-Kennebec-River." This old geography of place was not, however, without romance to some of us. To me the Amazon was something more than a line on the map. It was the highway to adventure. Ispahan was a city of rose-scented courts and dancing girls. The Sudan was a land of waving grass that all but hid herds of horned beasts. Walt Whitman in his "Salut au Monde" does a magnificent job of making places live. Once having visited a place, the mere mention of a name brings back a whole association of memories. For that reason I love the names of Ouray, Pacolet, Captiva, Korčula, Gabes and Isola Bella.

This knowing-of-place geography is, indeed, a proper beginning. A single issue of the Sunday New York *Times* was found by one of those singular, statistical minds to contain six hundred place names. "Everything that is, is somewhere." The spatial relationships are most important, but location is in itself no more geography than alphabetizing and spelling are literature. Of course, our geographies (they were big books, handy as a shield while eating candy) contained cultural oddities. All Eskimos apparently stood over a hole in the ice about to spear a fish. Somewhere in France shepherds followed herds across lagoons by using stilts. Dogs pulled milk carts in Holland. The knowledge Rebecca of Sunnybrook Farm had of the French was that they were fond of dancing and light wines. But these encyclopedic facts had no relation to each other except for accidents of locale. The child who was asked to name four animals of the Polar Zone (two seals and two polar bears) no more experienced an intellectual process than the classical student who was asked "Who dragged whom how many times around the walls of what?" (Supply the words: Achilles, Hector, three and Troy.) Even today our knowledge of foreign lands is often warped. Only recently did our elementary text book knowledge of China expand beyond the information which the New England sea captains brought back from their journeys to Canton for tea. Most people still do not know that the densely populated portion of Spain is rainy and heavily wooded. Too often the only book on Spain in our libraries is Washington Irving's description of Moorish life and art.

Those of us under forty years of age studied geography at a time when the texts were stiffened by statistics. The books, still large, taught the exact and misleading acreage of forest reserve in Alaska, misleading because there are very few trees and therefore few feet of timber per acre. Also given, was the place of the Belgian Congo as a producer of copper. But later our texts, elementary and college, began to deal more thoroughly with causal and therefore intellectual relationships. Writers are rapidly eliminating non-geographic material, such as comparative distances to the planets, the confusion of the international date line, and the fact that the Louvre is situated in Paris.

Modern geography has a simple definition, too simple to illustrate the exceptions: *Geography is the reciprocal relationship between physical environment and life.* Because of this there are metaphysical geographers who like to discuss whether or not there can be geography on a barren desert, or an Antarctic waste. The answer is: no life, no geography. If you accept the definition, then maps are not geography but only of geographic implication. A map of wheat is not a geographic map, nor is a map of rainfall, but put the facts of wheat and rainfall upon the same map so as to show the *relationship* and you have a geographic fact. Geographic facts always include cause and effect. One or the other, cause or effect, must have to do with the character of the physical environment. Limestone soils are basic in good corn production: geography. Pittsburgh had its beginnings because of the meeting of two rivers to form the easily navigable Ohio: geography. The Norwegians take to the sea because they live in a hunger land: geography. Dense agricultural populations decrease their standard of living as population increases: geography. Agriculture supports a greater density of population than a hunting and fishing culture: geography. But that Christ in Palestine preached the brotherhood of man, that Edison invented the moving picture in New Jersey, or that Germans are particularly musical, is not geography: there is no inter-relationship.

The word "reciprocal" in our definition of the word "geography" may have escaped your notice. This means that the environment may affect man, or that man may affect the environment. Immediately you rightly envis-age two schools of geographers according to the side of the relationship each may choose to stress. The elder school, beginning with the Greeks (so much begins with the Greeks), was of environmentalists, men who thought mostly in terms of the earth's influence on Man. The Middle Ages were barren except for the Arab, Ibn Khaldun, in the fourteenth century. Marco Polo, Toscanelli, Columbus, Magellan, Mercator and a thousand others were not geographers; they merely contributed to geographic knowledge. Throw in the names of Drake and Frobisher (or Admiral Byrd and Colonel Lindbergh), who were grand adventurers, but not primarily geographers. They were men of action rather than of philosophy.

In the period of Rationalism came Jean Bodin who saw, or thought he saw, the effect of climate on states, laws, religion, land, temperament and national char-acter. There was Montesquieu who philosophized upon environmentalism in his "Esprit des Lois," Taine with his interesting introduction to his "History of English Literature," and then Carl Ritter and his "Erdkunde." Nor can we overlook the biological environmentalists, Lamarck, Spencer, Darwin, and Haeckel.

Friedrich Ratzel of Berlin was the first systematic environmentalist in the anthropological field. It was a woman who brought the Ratzel system to America. No women were allowed in the classes of the University of Berlin, but a Louisville girl, Ellen Churchill Semple, sat just outside the door, and, challenged by the prejudice against sex, became his most distinguished pupil.* It was she who wrote: "Man is a product of the earth's surface. This means not merely that he is a child of the earth, dust of her dust; but that the earth mothered him, fed him, set him his tasks, directed his thoughts, confronted him with difficulties that have strengthened his body and sharpened his wits, given him his problems of navigation or irrigation, and at the same time whispered hints for their solution. She has entered in his bone and tissue." That is the thesis of her classic book. A grand philosophy when thought of sentimentally, and largely true, yet too embracing to withstand searching light. Modern geographers, lest they be more emotional than rational, have swung far from environmentalism as stated by Miss Semple. Without disowning the inspiration they took from environmentalism, they have naught to do with it in their current research.

Our modern rationalist hesitates to embrace environmentalism in his philosophy, partly because of the

* Miss Semple did the American edition of Ratzel, "Influences of Geographic Environment." She also gave us "Geographic Conditions in American History" and "Geography of the Mediterranean Region."

erroneous statements which have been so glibly made. For examples read the introduction to Henry Buckle's "History of English Civilization." Asiatics have short necks due to a habit of hunching up their shoulders because of the cold. This, of course, is cutting off the tail of a cow to make a tailless calf. Squint-eyed Chinese and black negroes were erroneously explained by the same faulty thinking. These misconceptions caused modern geographers to leave environmentalism to novelists and such loose-thinking fellows, and devote themselves entirely to man's effect upon the earth. Their geography was to be the story of man's adaptation of the environment to his purpose. They were landscapists, pure and simple. They talked about cultural landscape, terrene occupance, and sequence occupance. Fearful lest they be thought of as not scientific, they invented techniques by which to observe and analyze the details of a small region. They became, to use an old Greek word, chorographers.*

One can have no quarrel with chorographers as such. Indeed, your writer lists himself as one. Chorography is merely careful observation by means of certain techniques, the necessary preamble to conclusions. But chorographers are so concerned with listing provincial differences that often they are too exhausted to philosophize. However, they have rendered a great service to geography because they developed, and are devel-

* Topography is the study of a single slope, chorography the study of a small area, and geography is a broader view.

oping, a special set of observation techniques characteristic of geography alone. They wish to distinguish
geography from other subjects which, I am convinced,
is a mistake. This attempt at isolation of the subject
bears the same relation to what geography should be
as economic nationalism bears to a world-wide culture.
When they have completed their chorographic inventory they may have produced little more than a bigger
and better almanac. In pure chorography there is little
intellectual content. Chorography by itself is amoral.
It is good spelling, correct grammar, but in no sense
is it literature.

To many laymen, and, alas, to some geographers, it
will come as a shock that geography as a science is
neither fowl, fish nor good red herring. It has no important definitions of its own. It deals with no data not
already dealt with by some expert in another field.
What it is, is a correlation between sciences, and it is
only that. True, as a correlation it has a characteristic
technique, but that is a cause-and-effect rationalization.
If one *must* classify it, call it a philosophy.

Facts for geographic philosophy come from too many
sciences, physical and social, to list. Geology, agronomy,
botany, zoology, agriculture, anthropology, sociology,
history, economics, and business, all furnish factual
grist for the geographer's mill, whether he lean to the
environmentalist's or the chorographer's school. It
makes a congress of geographers more or less a Committee on the Universe. A large order, this treating of

cabbages and kings, cathedrals and linguistics, trade in
oil, or commerce in ideas. One must grant *some* limitations to the geographer's peregrinations, so metaphysics
and abstract philosophy are out. Modestly the geographer does not explain the universal concept of a god-
head.

Much of the geographer's field you are to be spared.
There are many more expert chorographers than your
author, and this little volume is largely only a defense
of the almost-discarded environmentalism.

So much by way of introducing our subject. Because
it is written by a professor it need not lose for you the
romance of far-away places and the edge of things. A
geographer, though he be academic, may yet love the
cerulean blue of a glacier's crevasse. He may laugh at
the sight of a Breton girl, her ample *jupe* flowing in
the wind, riding a bicycle while wearing wooden shoes.
He may look upon the spacious scenes of Peter Fleming's "News from Tartary" as the reality of "Lost Horizon." In truth, though a professor, he may be a thoroughly human geographer. If little is known of modern
geography, less indeed is known of those strange fellows, the geographers. Of course, they are much concerned with statistics but they are, it is agreed, also
travelers. How then do they differ from the ordinary
traveler?

A facetious definition of geography which is not
without worth is that geography is what geographers
do. In other words, judge all men by their works. I

don't know what many geographers do exactly, nor can I be responsible for their acts. But I am sure wise geographers go into the field. Though there may be first an arm chair period when they read about a land, in the end they must travel to foreign parts and perhaps stay to map their discoveries in detail. This mapping is the aforementioned chorography.

Ordinarily our studies are not so painstaking. The geographer travels to check and observe. He wants to know *how* hot and humid jungles are. He wants to see the tidal maelstrom off the Lofoten Islands. He wants to survey Tibetan passes, or actually measure the volume of trade on the Rhine. Only thus can he write or teach convincingly. Only after being on the spot is he near conviction of the facts of others, or of his own theories.

How does the geographer travel? More likely than not he remains in one place for some time to sense that undercurrent of environmental influence. It is only thus that he realizes the significance of physical environment in the life of the people. He is able then to analyze the features of the landscape and, in turn, show the role of each in the development of culture. What to the ordinary traveler is merely a contrast of picturesque habits in several sections of a country becomes to the geographer cultural differentiation based upon provincial contrasts. He comes to understand the origin of ways of living and the origin of ways of thinking. He finds the true reason for the agricultural habits of Spain. He comes to understand the melancholy of Scottish folk-songs from their setting in a peat-smoke-filled hut in a fog-drenched land with the oats ruined for lack of sun.

Now the geographer is often concerned with more technical analyses than sensing provincial cultures. In-

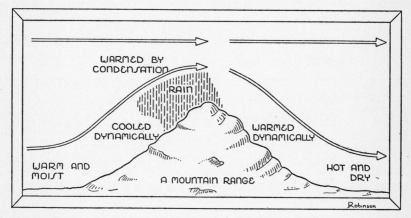

Fig. 1. Diagram to explain the Föhn wind. Now read the text again and your mental atmosphere will clear.

deed, frequently he is so concerned with technicalities that he misses the quality of life. Problems of urban geography, transportation, statistics of production, and classifications of soils come before him for solution. Let me present one rather simple technicality, that of the *Föhn* wind. In America it is known as the Chinook wind, the snow eater. The physics of the *Föhn* is this: as air rises to upper levels it expands and so cools; as it descends the far side of a mountain it is compressed and warmed. Therefore, it should arrive on the lee plain with the same temperature it had on the plain of origin. But, if in rising it causes rain to form through cooling, the heat liberated by the process of condensation prevents the full degree of cooling which would be expected during the ascent. Descending on the far side of the mountain it must be warmed. Therefore, at the station in the lee of the mountain the wind arrives much hotter and drier than on the plain of origin. Whether or not this explanation be clear, let me assure you that *Föhn* wind is so hot and gusty as to destroy your nerves, and so dry that certain Alpine villages have restrictions against building hearth fires as long as such a wind blows, lest the village burn.

But this wind dries and sweetens the soil in spring and brings crops to flower and harvest. The grape of the Swiss and Austrian valleys is found only on those slopes exposed to the *Föhn*. In such an exposure is produced the famous Swiss wine, *fondant de Sion*. The Austrians say that two hours of *Föhn* are worth two weeks of sunshine.

The geographer, like any other interested traveler, seeks to know as much as possible about a land before his visit. Fortunately, his knowledge is limited and he, too, has the joy of exploration. I had been in Carinthia, in southern Austria, where I was investigating a phenomenon known as an inversion of temperature, and where I could climb in the Karawanken Alps. The other side of this range was Yugoslavia, about which I knew as much as I do of Tanganyika. So to Slovenia and Croatia and Dalmatia went I, open-mouthed at the new house types, the picturesque methods of drying hay, the girl herders of geese, the fertility of the Save Valley, the wildness of the forests, and the rapid growth of such cities as Llubjiana and Zagreb. It was Louis Adamic's "The Native's Return" in reality.

This is all apropos of the beginning of a search for warmth, and illustrates how an unexpected factor may change the course of travel. Nowhere in winter in Croatia, Slovenia, or Carniola was warmth to be found. But as our train crossed the divide of the Dalmatian Alps and descended the Adriatic slope, warmth pervaded our bodies. Here, I believe, is one of the most decisive climatic boundaries in Europe. And, if you travel with a geographer, you learn that the stone walls on the north side of the track as you cross the divide are there to keep the fierce *bora* * wind from blowing the train from the rails.

Dalmatia has always been one of the hotbeds of struggle in Europe. Here, there is an opportunity for illustrating the geographer's greatest interest in travel, political geography. Here, two geographic principles oppose each other. There is a principle that a rich agricultural interior like the Save Valley strives for ports on the sea. The ports on the Adriatic are reached only after crossing the Dalmatian Alps, and the Adriatic littoral is so independent as to have almost a separatist

---

* A *bora* wind is like a *mistral*. It is the sudden downward release of a mass of cold air accumulated upon a plateau.

tendency from the interior. But there is a second geographic principle at work. It is an axiom of geography that an enclosed sea, much as a peninsula, has a tendency to come politically and culturally under the dominant power which borders its waters. The Adriatic, after Julius Caesar's time, became Roman. Later, Diocletian actually established his imperial palace on the Dalmation shore, from which he gave slight attention to matters of state, and great attention to his cabbage patch. Then Venice dominated both shores and gave architectural ideas to the town of Korčula. Italians have spread to the Dalmatian shores, and today Italian political claims follow. Italy took Trieste and the Istrian shore from Austria. So ungeographic a move was this that Trieste threatened to have grass in the streets like the cities Hoover foresaw if the Democratic regime ever won. Italy took the ports of Fiume and Zara from Yugoslavia, Italy lent a vast sum to poor Albania which that country will never be able to repay, and now Italy has foreclosed on the mortgage.

So here are two principles of geography working counter to each other. Their comparative strength is shown at Fiume. Previous to the war, Fiume was the terminus of the single railway crossing the Dalmatian Alps. Since, two others have been built. The Italians, seizing Fiume, stifled trade there, but one suburb of that city, Sušak, and a small portion of the harbor, were left to Yugoslavia. When I saw the spacious harbor it held but two vessels, one of which was a gunboat. On the other hand, the little harbor of Sušak was inadequate to berth the thirty or forty vessels that crowded the basin.

So the geographer travels for discovery and exploration, he travels to analyze the settings of cultural developments, he travels to find the answer to problems to which otherwise only a theoretical answer would be available, and, like everyone else, he travels for sheer joy. Geography must be looked upon not as an old-fashioned matter of national boundaries and the location of capital cities, but as a living subject, full of the variety of human life, which explains ways of living in all their myriad diversity. Geography should be, and is, grand fun.

Chapter Two

A GEOGRAPHIC

PHILOSOPHY

T HE TURNING WHEEL," BY STUART CLOETE IS A
story of the Dutch and their migrations under English
pressure to new lands in the veldt of South Africa.
These are the descendants, not far removed, of the
tillers of the *polder* lands at the mouth of the Rhine.
The novelist would say that they had in their blood
the placidity of the cheese makers of the Netherlands.
True, it was the most adventurous of these that chose
to be migrants. But, once on the perilous veldt, these
Boers became another people. Fighters they were,
ruthless pioneers. Sex with them was no longer merely

34

family; it was a strong passion. Their minds were those
of the beasts of the field. What was it that changed
the quiet Dutch farmers into fierce Boers? Was this
new spirit the result of the environment? The answer
is convincing to all who read the book. Here is grand
environmentalism, but is the environmentalism deterministic?

Brooks Adams in his "The New Empire" says, "It
may be that all human affairs are determined.... But
the law of that determinism has not been disclosed;
and no effort of the positivists, no matter how pro-
longed, assiduous and eager, can establish it." All this
is true "because it is known that untold numbers of
events in the past, which must be included as relevant
parts of any alleged deterministic sequence, are unknown and cannot be known because of the fragmentary character of historical data available." The first
statement is, of course, true. We behave as we behave
because we have no choice. A series of conditioning
events have led us to make in a predetermined fashion
a decision or an invention. We love or hate because
of a complex of already historical events. But Adams
is speaking of determinism in general, whereas in this
volume determinism is used to mean control of our
lives by physical environment.

This concept of determinism, if it be true, is especially
difficult for an American to understand because, essentially, he has no locale. The Iowa farmer in the winter
may be found playing shuffleboard in Miami. Air-

planes and streamlined trains bring one coast close to
the other, and many people live their lives far removed
from the place of their upbringing.* But let generation
after generation become fixed and there is a continuity
of culture which becomes traditional. We are prone to
talk about our inherited characteristics, but physical
characteristics are socially of slight importance as compared with cultural inheritance. In the old world there
is what is known as the peasant attitude towards life.
This is, in reality, the inheritance of the physical circumstance of locale, the result of fixity. The greater the
duration of fixity the longer has environment an opportunity to work its slow, almost gentle, but always
persistent influence.

To illustrate this factor of fixity let me tell a story
of a traveler who asked a Chinese the way to a nearby
village.

The Traveler: "The village lies just beyond the hill,
does it not?"

The Chinese: "I believe so."

* If one wishes an exquisite example of the importance of a
native heath in the development of imagination, read Alain-
Fournier's "The Wanderer," translated by Francoise Delisle
from "Le Grand Meaulnes." It is a story of, to use Fournier's
words, "the country of my dreams—the country from which I
am exiled." Havelock Ellis in the introduction speaks of this
land, the Sologne in Central France, as "a land of alders, rushes,
and reeds, in a horizon which recalls the miniatures in the old
French Books of Hours with their delicate pinnacles against the
sky. It was the region which alone Fournier knew in early life
and it made on him a profound impression." This is one of
those eerie pieces of literature which once read never leaves you.
It is another "Green Mansions" in its delicacy.

The Traveler: "Don't you know? Don't you live here?"

The Chinese: "I don't know about the village. I live *here.*" And he pointed to the ground beneath him.

It is this exclusive association with one's personal cabbage patch, vineyard, or rice paddy that permits the full development of the peasant frame of mind. Louis Adamic magnificently portrays the peasant when he describes his native village near Llubjiana in Yugoslavia. In an article in *Harpers Magazine* he tells of death in Carniola. He describes how his Uncle Yanez returned to the soil, and it was no more strange to the villagers than the plowing under of summer's stubble, or the falling of the leaves. It vindicates in part the quotation of Semple given you in the first chapter, her famous dust-to-dust statement.

Adamic's mother speaks of the passing of her brother Yanez with a sense of fatalism. This perplexed Adamic until he discovered the whole village took the fact of death in the same manner. His father said, "Sooner or later we must all go to the long home, just as the dew goes before the sun. Do you remember the big apple tree that grew in the middle of the meadow this side of the creek?"

Adamic did, and his father went on to say, "Two or three years ago, when spring came, that apple tree did not bloom or leaf. It was just an old tree, mostly hollow inside, and it died. People become hollow inside and go the same way."

In "The Native's Return" Adamic writes again of Slovene life and death. He shows how these people, long-rooted to place, preserved their pagan beliefs. He says, "This whole village appears to be in deep harmony with the region. It is an indigenous part of it. And these people belong here as much as these swallows flying about. They are intimate with their surroundings. They know what their function is without ever really thinking about it. Death is only a part, an inevitable incident in that intimacy with their environment; and, like other incidents in their lives, they have glossed it over with poetry and semi-religious beliefs...."

This being in harmony with one's physical habitat is by some curious chance better understood by travelers and fiction writers than by geographers who should have a special claim on such facts. The geographers are so much concerned with chorographic technicalities that few of them could spare the time to write such beautiful culture descriptions as did Nora Waln in "Grape Harvest," in the *Atlantic Monthly*.* These happy descriptions of life in the German Ahr Valley, and the writings of Adamic, are the products of philosophers who sense the human scheme rather than the prosaic analysis which the academic geographer makes. The professional geographer is always cluttering up his work desk with new tools. He has left neither time nor space in which to work. The tools

* October, 1937.

must be sharpened, classified and given new names. When that is finished it is time for bed.

But it still remains that when environment is a passive agent it cannot be deterministic. All geographers are ready, too ready, to subscribe to this. This would be completely true if physical environment were always constant. But it is known that physical environment is not constant. In changing, environment alters the limitations by which culture is defined and even forces new economics upon us. The sea changes the coast. The moor upon which Shakespeare set the scene of Lear's mad wandering in the night has been eroded away. There were recently published pictures of the once-pleasant resort of Fire Island as a broken, desert waste because of a hurricane. Soil is a function of climate. Let the climate change and any one of a number of things may happen to the soil. Let the man who scorns the possibility of determinism remember the Dust Bowl, read Sears' "Deserts on the March," and weep at the weakness of man.

Here is a part of a letter from a woman who lived on the edge of the Dust Bowl in 1936:

"As far as you can see in any direction from our place there is nothing but black dirt, not a tree, not a shrub, not even a Russian thistle. High drifts of dirt are piled around the house and the woven fence enclosing the yard is half-buried in loose silt. Hardly a spear of grass is visible within a radius of a mile from the ranch. During the past dry hot summer the cattle nibbled every blade down to the roots as they came into water at the dam below the house. Not even in the early spring was there any green to be seen on the prairies. The grasshoppers ate the fresh blades of grass as soon as it pushed up out of the earth. No rain fell after the snows melted in March and the only feed left in our pasture is the cured hay from summer before last.

"Not one mouthful of feed was put up on the ranch this summer. The only roughage we have for wintering our cattle is eighty tons of oatstraw left over from last year. This fall my husband sold all of his calves, the dry cows and the two-year-old heifers so that all we have to winter are the steers and the she-stuff that should have calves in the spring. The cattle left are strong but they are thin and their coats look rougher than I have seen them in years. They are still 'rustling' for feed in our pasture south of here. Toward evening, they come stringing into the sheds and my husband hauls out oil cake for them. He hopes there will be no snow until February so they can get their roughage from the pasture until then. He has leased a place down on the Missouri River where he will move them when the feed in the pasture is covered up. The brakes along the river offer protection against the cold winds and he has bought a two-year stack of alfalfa hay and several loads of Russian thistles. This he hopes will keep them going until March when he will bring them up

here on the flat and feed them the oatstraw which he
is now so jealously guarding.

"Well, this may be, as my optimistic friends out here
are prophesying, a 'good year' and *if* snow holds off
until February, and *if* we have an early spring with

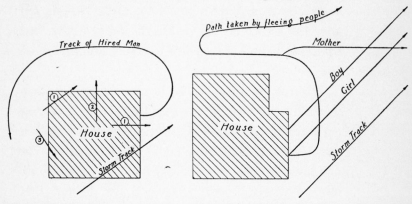

Fig. 2. Flight diagram of victims of geographic determinism
during two tornadoes, showing actual paths through air of
the victims of the storms.

enough rain to start the grass and *if* the prices of beef
stay up, we'll get enough from the sale of the steers we
are holding over to put us out of the red. No one ever
wins who does not gamble a bit. The stakes are high
this year but there was no alternative. All of our neighbors who have not left the country are taking the same
chances and few of them have as good a pasture as we
have but as I go around and talk to the people I never
hear a discouraging word. Everyone is talking about
the 'good year' we are bound to have 'next year.' "

Whether or not this letter describes determinism

or near-determinism depends upon one's definition of the word. Certainly catastrophic geography, even to the purists, must be considered deterministic. Tornadoes, earthquakes, or volcanic eruptions are all forms of intense environment. The lives and perhaps deaths of the farmer, the farmer's wife and the hired man, as represented in the diagram, were determined.

Can we weigh the influences on man's life? They are, of course, imponderable, yet we can speak of strong or weak genetic factors, or strong or weak environmental factors. In a like fashion, we can give an approximation of the importance of man's choice or will in determining an event. All three factors, inheritance, environment, and human volition, are variables. It is as unlikely that any of these variables should be eliminated in computing the totality of forces leading to an event as it would be to consider any of them as being singly responsible. If the variables be X, Y and Z, we cannot give to X a hundred percent significance without reducing Y and Z to zero.

If we conceive all events as having spatial relations within a cube, and if we consider one corner as having a zero value, the three dimensions might each stand for an increase in the force of one of the three variables. Here look at the cube in the diagram. Let the X dimension stand for the increasing genetic factor in the character of an individual, Y may be considered the environmental factor, and Z the voluntary factor. What is then the make-up of any individual can be plotted within the cube. Or any historical event may be shown spatially. In that case, let X equal the sequence of events leading to a point in time, Y equals the envi-

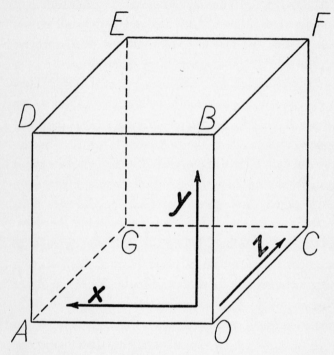

Fig. 3. If **x** is increasing control by inheritance, **y** the environmental factor in one's life, and **z** the increase of human choice in any event, any fact relating to man's action may be plotted within the cube.

ronmental influences found at the place of the event, and Z equals the human voluntary influences upon that event. Events of a physical catastrophe would lie along the line O-B. The diagram has the single virtue of illustrating that though there is a slight possibility of the almost complete diminution of two of the variables, there is also a possibility, though slight, of an approach to domination of one variable ever the other two.

A definition tells what a thing is and, by giving its limitations, tells what it is not. Of course, geographers in a congress are not really a Committee on the Universe. Let me now more seriously declare some decided limits of environmentalistic thought. Obviously, most of the cultural landscape is the direct choice of man. It is true that New York got its start because it had an excellent harbor with access to the rich Northwest Territory through the Mohawk corridor. But after that has been said, the chief elements of environmental influence on the development of New York have been presented.* Geography of production has to do with distribution. Urban geography has to do largely with redistribution. Indeed, the cultural landscape of New York has little to do with the local environment. Buildings tower to unbelievable heights. They are made of steel, stone, cement, brick, and tile, none of which comes from the metamorphic rocks that underlie Manhattan Island. People travel above the ground. People travel underground. The electricity they use is developed from coal, and their automobiles are driven with gasoline, neither

* This is, in fact, something of an overstatement. My bibliography mentions ten articles on the geography of New York including the interesting article "The Water Barriers of New York City" by Ellsworth Huntington, *Geographical Review,* Vol. II (1916), pp. 169-183.

of which is discoverable in Manhattan, nor anywhere near Manhattan. Buildings are air-conditioned to maintain a monotonous 72 degrees the year around. Broadway is brilliantly lit at midnight, turning night into day. People live on streets which rarely receive direct sunlight, and go to clinics to get sun-tanned. The environment is man-made. Seasons, almost day and night, are eliminated. Is it true that sheep and cattle are actually carted around to the schools so that children may know that wool does not originate in a sweat shop and milk in cans? New York is a grand place for the urban chorographer but no place for the geographic environmentalist; natural milieu is everywhere thrust aside by sociology and city engineering.

Perhaps the greater the modernity the less the local environmentalism. But whatever New Yorkers think, New York is not basic in our national culture. Everything that is fundamental in New York began somewhere else. Steel that comes from Pittsburgh, cement from the Lehigh Valley, wheat from the Dakotas, and rum from Cuba, all make New York what it is. That man with the hoe or the miner with a pick made New York possible. Such workers are rooted in the earth, and each is using the earth in an intimate fashion. Culture *begins* in the paths between the corn, in the forest lane, or along the mine tracks, and flows to New York, where it undergoes a metamorphism. Support of environmentalism is more easily found in the lives of those bound down to soil and place, those who live

according to the dictates of nature, and not those who
live in New York.

These dictates of place are much less in number than
one would at first imagine.* There is little in, say, a
Michigan landscape that determines what is grown
there. True, coconuts can not be produced about De-
troit, and there are few wild elephants that survive the
Michigan winter. But Henry Ford promises fair to
change much of the agricultural scene, so far have his
agents gone in proving the value of certain new farm
crops for industrial purposes. Some of the subjects of
one of the Dearborn conferences were: making alcohol
from farm products; introduction of the cork and *tung*
tree (*tung* oil is used in varnish); corn grown for
starches and sugar; oats as a cosmetic, as a preservative
for coffee, for cleaning oils and gasoline; farm products
of many sorts for plastics; whole cotton as a source of
oil; soy beans in the paint industry, and soy beans as
a food.

It is possible that the farm product will soon substi-
tute for many of our mineral industries. We are only
to a slight extent limited by minerals, soil and climate.

* Under the title of "Good-Bye Good Earth" (*Readers Digest,*
1938) we have about the last word on artificiality. Wake Island
is a low, sterile, almost rainless island which lies far west of the
Hawaiian Islands. It is a landing place for the China Clipper,
a way station with nothing to recommend it but its remarkable
location. The invention of growing plants in chemically treated
water has been transferred to the strand of Wake. Now trans-
Pacific passengers obtain fresh vegetables from the tank gardens.
This is unreasonable and, to the environmentalist, quite unjust.

Man has an opportunity of adapting earth products to his purpose limited only by his inventiveness. How man, rather than resources, determines economies is shown in the common misconception that the presence of coal in England is responsible for her industrial development. Not at all. Coal gives the possibility of industrialism, but does not determine it. China for centuries had coal under each of her eighteen provinces, yet, until the twentieth century, she had no steam industry, though coal had been used there for heating since the days of Marco Polo.

It is true that necessity is the mother of invention. Over-population, which is a geographic fact, is one of the great necessities which has promoted invention. When considering the character of invention we must, however, always remember the human factor. There is no reason why any two peoples living under exactly the same geographic conditions should have a similar form of inventiveness. The Chinese invented gunpowder; the English, a steam engine. Of course, as geographers, we should like to have similar responses to similar environments, which we call parallel cultural evolution. Examples of such parallelism in culture are, as a matter of fact, rare, and then only partial.

England and Japan have much in common physically. Both are groups of islands with considerable area and variety of resources. Both are in regions of energizing climate. Both are just off continents. And both received their culture from the mainland, which in each case has undergone a modification that represents a provincialism. This is true of the language, for example. And the Japanese form of Buddhism bears approximately the same relation to continental Buddhism as the Anglican church bears to the Roman church. Being islands, both suffered over-population. Both have an intense provincialism which expressed itself first in nationalism and then in the form of a cultural, as well as a military imperialism. Both have turned to industrialism and mercantilism to solve food problems. But in the end, there are so many differences between the two peoples, such obvious differences, that one refrains from listing them. Were the Japanese to trade places with the English we would hardly expect them also to exchange approaches to national problems.

Indeed, the human element in culture is often greater than the physical factor. Man brings to any region an "impact of culture" * which represents his group's approach to life. Gaul, under the Romans, was assuming an orderly agriculture. With the invasions of the barbarians, civilization devolved and a hunting and a herding culture was imposed on the land. Roads decayed. Cities were replaced by camps fortified by mud walls. This was the impact of the barbarians' culture, an impact which took centuries to overcome. The physical circumstance, then, was far less important than traditional culture.

We even have people living lives opposed to the so-

* Gordon East's, "Historical Geography of Europe."

called dictates of environment. Tundra lands are those areas in regions where the mean annual temperature is below freezing, where the subsoil is continually frozen and the heat of summer is only sufficient to thaw the surface soil. In the summer time such areas are given over to grasses. Trees do not grow because their roots need to reach down into the frozen zone. Ice does not support vegetation, and the great expanses of grass lands are solitary to an overwhelming degree. Since the surface water can not seep away through the ice, vast areas are given over to swamp, and mosquitoes. In winter time the tundras are covered with a relatively light covering of snow. Reindeer, having large hooves, find it possible to paw through the snow to find evergreen mosses and lichens for food; you know how in our woods the Christmas fern remains green all winter. Other herbivorous animals feed in the same fashion, but the reindeer is the only similar beast domesticated. So, in the tundras of Eurasia, the domesticated reindeer is a logical basis of human economy. We presume that the tundra people of Asia were originally from the grassy, treeless steppes. This presumption is because primitives do not easily change environments. Forest people come to live on moors or grass lands only when compelled to do so. The tundra people apparently came from the open steppes; they have legends of owning horses, and their priests embroider steppe flowers on their robes. Do not the llamas of dry Tibet use the water-loving lotus flower as a religious symbol?

In the eastern Asian tundras live the Yakuts, who were steppe people. On the original steppe lands they were cattle herders. Having come to the tundra lands they prefer to raise cattle rather than reindeer. But the cattle do not eat moss and lichen and in winter must be fed upon hay gathered in the summer, so the short summer season is a period of feverish human activity. During the long days of the solstice, the people strive desperately to provide hay. Failure means a decline of winter milk and starvation. So meager is the margin of safety that families give way to economic units, several workers and some old or young that tend the cattle. The strongest worker, perhaps a young girl, may be the head of the economic "family." Let the food supply fail in winter, and she can force a parent to walk out into the storm to find death. Here is an impact which has made the people environmental misfits.

The failure of geographic environment greatly embarrasses me in my thesis. Civilization's progress has been defined as a people's intelligence in adapting the earth's surface to its purpose. By such a standard these people are less civilized than the naked bushman of the South African desert; the bushmen at least have made the most of what they have.

Or again, there are the people of the oases of Suf in the western Sahara. This portion of the Sahara is sandy, and most deserts, of course, have little or no sand. The oases are holes in the sand reaching down to a clay base where is found sufficient ground water to support the palm tree, barley, vegetables and ground fruits. But the water supply is precarious and some years is less than what is needed. Moreover, each year the shifting sands move in upon the hollows. Each year the people carry out the sand in a desperate effort to preserve their fields. It is, of all the places in the world where agriculture is at all possible, one of the least attractive, an agriculture in spite of nature. As one approaches, only the tops of the date palms can be seen. The farmers of the Suf have practically buried themselves in the desert. They live in unstable sand quarries, which does not make sense geographically.

In short, there are definite limitations to the use of physical phenomena as the causal explanation of social habits and institutions. The anthropologist is quick to reply to so confirmed an environmentalist as myself by showing how quite similar environments, or even the same environment, will support widely different cultures. Lucien Febvre in his "Geographical Introduction to History" has written a philippic against environmentalism. We have geographers of limited philosophy in our very midst who will have nothing to do with environmental factors, but that is their naïve privilege.

Sorokin in his contemporary "Sociological Theories" takes the stand that any particularistic, deterministic explanation of a phenomenon is false. He contends that all factors in creating the phenomenon are interdependent and interact upon one another. No one factor is ever a full explanation. In other words, he would permit the plotting of no historical event on the edge of our cube. With this I would like to agree to maintain a reputation for moderation, but again and again in this study of environmentalism, it delights me to place events in the cube so near to the environmental edge as to reduce to a minimum the other two variables. Of course, I could write a book about genetics, or human initiative, and lay emphasis on facts in other parts of the cube. Rationally, I dare not claim to be an environmental determinist, but I cannot entirely exclude such a philosophy.

Chapter Three

UNDERSTANDING

EVOLUTION

THIS IS A VOLUME ABOUT ENVIRONMENTALISM. IF I SEEM to scorn those authors who fail to credit environment with its true importance, then, in justice and of necessity, I must expose the significance of the genetic factor. The theory of evolution is not difficult to understand but unfortunately there is not a little in evolution that, as yet, is explained by no theory. Also, not every one will today accept the word "evolution" in good standing. These are often people with small vocabularies. But if for "evolution" is substituted the word "change," the matter is simple. An irate farmer member of the Legislature's Finance Committee complained that this heretical doctrine was being taught at Ohio State University. He voiced his anger to the dean of agriculture. The dean rather casually took him to the horse barns and they discussed horse breeding. It came over the man that he was himself talking evolution. It is as simple as that.

There was mighty opposition to Darwin's fine thinking in the mid-nineteenth century. There came the famous man-from-monkey controversy. It was only a few years ago that the splendid but pitiful Bryan was raging at the Dayton, Tennessee, evolution trial. I do not know whether Bryan lived long enough to learn of the girl child born shortly after the trial only a few miles from Dayton with a spinal appendage several inches long. These vestigial tails occasionally happen. They are cut off: sitting and dressmaking difficulties require it. There is a man who collects them; he is reported to have twenty-five of them. Charming hobby!

But this is not the place to write a defense of evolution. It would bore my intelligent readers and I don't think that the anti-evolutionists read books. Ontogeny and recapitulation * of the race, knowledge of the human embryo, and even casual observation, are proof enough of that almost systematic progress and change

* Ontogeny is the history of evolution of individual organisms, and recapitulation refers to the theory that the stages through which the embryo passes represent steps in the organism's evolution.

which we call evolution. The methods of evolution are, however, here important.

Even the Greeks accepted evolution for man. Only the gods sprang "full-armed from the head of Zeus." But one of the first theorists was Buffon (1707-1788). He had the idea that plants were molded directly by *environment*. Lamarck later stressed function. New wants were said to result in new organs. He is the only man, then, who can explain how the cow developed the cud stomach or the camel its hump. Along came Goethe. He was a Romanticist. He said there was "growth force towards self-realization." This might work with the remarkable *Homo sapiens* who by his own confession has a soul, but what about the growth-force-towards-self-realization of an oyster?

It was the systematic Darwin who gave us our first light on method. He created the idea of natural selection. As stated by geographers, all life, human as well, must pass through environmental screens. Those that do not fit the interstices are eliminated. To be almost too simple, deer in the forest have small horns compared with deer on the plains or moors. The deer of the plains have large horns to give them an advantage in fighting. But large horns on the deer in the forest catch in the branches so the animals fall prey to the wolves. Forest deer that live to reproduce a race are small-horned. This is evolution by selection. Thus environment aids in selecting. Races or groups of men that have made long and dangerous treks lasting through a number of generations eliminate the physically weak and the mentally unfit as they pass through the environmental screens. Such groups end up superior races. We are told that one half the passengers on the *Mayflower* died the first year. Four-fifths of the Jamestown settlers died or returned home in the first years.

Natural selection was not sufficient to explain the new varieties and changes in life forms. De Vries then classified the unexplained changes under the head of mutants. If a bed of white primroses produce a pink primrose and that primrose produces an unchanging series of generations of pinks then one has a mutant. It is a variation that becomes a permanent variety. New England, in less modern times, had only stone walls. The sheep jumped these walls with ease. In the course of biologic change a ram was born that had short legs, so short that he could not jump the walls. Our ram was a persistent mutant. All its descendants had short legs. It must have been a virile ram for it bred a whole race of sheep. These sheep, none of them, could jump the walls. A new variety had come into existence.

The questions of life progress in genera and species are not yet all answered. Nor can we always guess what part of evolution is determined by heredity and what part by selection. The horse was once a five-toed animal. Being a beast of the plain without good defense its preservation lay in acquiring speed. Literally it got up on its toes, and finally on one toe. Those individuals who did not do so were killed. The development of the middle toe for speed seems a selective process, but the failure of the lateral toes may well have been mutation. A disused organ disappears only in so far as it is a hindrance to life, unless it goes out through the mutant process. We carry about with us some seventy vestigial organs most of which are dead weight: the appendix, tonsils, the membrane in the corner of the eye, the vertebrate sections (tail) at the end of the spinal column beyond the pelvic bone, and the hair that curves around the fore arm. Now the appendix we seem always to have with us. It may some day disappear through mutation, or it may become smaller since those who have large appendices will have them inflamed and so die. Of course, today we dash these misformed people off to the hospital, save their lives and allow them to reproduce offspring with large or larger appendices. This is grand business for the doctor. A less sentimental and more eugenic race would either shoot or sterilize people with large appendices. In short, civilization is defeating evolution. We not only preserve the physically unfit but the mentally unfit. Lady Bountiful and the Community Fund strive with religious zeal to permit every mentally inefficient family to have as many babies as possible. Clinics for birth control are the greatest benefactors of the human race that we have. Let us pray for worthy mutations rather than physicians for under our present system the human race is not evolving and perhaps is deteriorating.

We have yet to dispose of the doctrine of acquired characteristics. Restated it is: if the Indians living high in the Andes develop huge lungs with which to gain sufficient oxygen from the rarefied air then gradually lung capacity will increase in the offspring and so become a group characteristic. De Vries and the friar Mendel believed such. A certain Weismann refuted them. As late as 1915 L. M. Bristol in his "Social Adaptation" suggested that environment was the vital influence in variations and organic evolution. Are we never going to lay the ghost of the cow with the clipped tail giving birth to a calf without a tail, or at least with a tail a little bit shorter? *

In spite of refutations, learned scientists talk about the adaptability of life forms. We do have, as humans, a wide range of adaptability. Men live in Nova Zembla amid stultifying cold, meagerness of resources and monotony of landscape. Men live in Kalgoorlie in the Australian desert, where water is brought in pipes for two hundred miles, and the heat of the land makes life in the mine tunnels a relief. We have ranges of adaptability but beyond limits we cannot go. Madison Grant says race sets the limit: "As measured in terms of centuries, unit characters are immutable and the only benefit to be derived from a changed environment and

---

* As a matter of fact it has been found that apparently experiences within the life cycle of one generation can be transmitted to the behavior of a second generation in the lower forms of animals. This is, of course, disconcerting to the dogmatists. See Sanders' "Environment and Growth."

better food conditions is the opportunity afforded a race which has lived under adverse conditions to achieve its maximum development, but the limits of that development are fixed for it by heredity and not by environment." This is true, of course, only if the life cycle is fulfilled in one place and that place have an unchanged environment. There is, however, a great deal of human migration and we know that climates change and soils erode. The everlasting hills are not unchanging.

There are still many sides of evolution unexplained. Where do behavior patterns, that is, instincts, come from? And how does one insect know that at a certain season by stinging another insect in a certain portion of the body the first insect can there lay its eggs and so preserve its kind? Whence the intelligence of birds that, after mating, build a nest?

Is it possible that experiences of the race are crowded into the early mental development even as we see the early physical stages of the race crowded into the embryo? Millenniums in nine months! I am not adverse to thinking of social as well as physical recapitulation. Are social habits as love, the mating instinct, or the nest-building urge developed as psychological mutations or by selection, or as acquired characteristics? Is it entirely a humorous report that women know when a baby is about to arrive because they discover themselves cleaning long-neglected closets? Try asking people if a little girl left on a desert island would find a stick for a doll and so express the maternal instinct. Psychologists will be almost insulted in declaring "no" but a bit of mystical Irish in my blood (a very unscientific statement) makes me give credence to folk ways. Call this social recapitulation, if you wish to be technical. The evidences of social evolution have a time-honored surge to them that carries strength. It is probably true, for example, that food-collecting habits do not arise in the individual but are the result of generations of experience. No method of evolution has been formulated by which we may account for them.

It is true that the history of a genus of life forms is a cycle of more or less complete adaptation to environment. We know that heredity always has an environmental setting—no seed flourishes without a congenial soil. But that there must be a relation between the plant and the soil does not necessarily give to the plant a quality of adaptability. If we believe in natural selection do we not necessarily believe that life has not the adaptive quality? Nor is there anything geographical in mutants. Mutation is merely the inherent quality to vary. Largely by this process the world has progressed from homogeneity to heterogeneity. But if we do not know what causes mutants, we do know that the environmental screen has much to do with determining what mutants are to continue existence. That evolution is not always adaptive, is shown by the progress of certain characteristics which have finally caused the extinction of a whole order. The dinosaurs may well be a case in point. It is believed that the dinosaur developed so much bulk of body without an increase of brain space that the stupid hulk was easily preyed upon by other beasts. We have some ornate sea cephalopods of the geologic past which by extension of their shells actually shut off the possibility of existence.

Genetics and biology are tremendously interesting studies because we have not yet all the answers. But enough has been said to show that realism in evolution involves the selective screen of environment. Here is something concrete. Here is the geographical factor in history. In many cases physical evolution presents problems for which there is as yet no plausible theory. When we come to social evolution we have a third variable introduced. This is man's will. The direction of leadership or genius is frequently far beyond the scope of geography. Gertrude Stein is reported to have told our confident friend, Robert M. Hutchins, president of the University of Chicago, that professors (and, one presumes, Mr. Hutchins) were not interesting to a degree that they had all the answers. You now witness one professor who states that the interest in his subject is in a large part in the unanswered questions. To write upon a subject in which I had all the answers would bore me. Controversy and speculation keep the blood circulating.

Chapter Four

ENVIRONMENT IN

THE PAST

THE STORY OF MAN SHOULD COMMENCE WITH THE first protoplasm for it was then that our traits began. But we shall have to take up our story with the opening of the Cambrian Period. The geologic Cambrian Period is the first or earliest of the sedimentary periods of rock formation. The table which we reproduce for you shows older rocks (we sometimes call them basement rocks) to be largely metamorphic, which means that they have been so pressed and contorted as to have lost their original form. That life existed in the pre-Cambrian period we know because of graphite and the calcareous content of the formations. Free carbon and calcium carbonate are, so far as we know, the result of organic processes.

The Cambrian rocks were laid down in great continental salt water seas, say, a matter of five hundred million years ago. With the first Cambrian rocks appears the fossil of a trilobite, a superior animal not unlike a crayfish. The trilobite, dragging his belly about in the mud, was nevertheless king of all he surveyed. The last word is used advisedly for he had an eye of a thousand parts. Indeed, trilobites had most of the sensory organs with which we are equipped. This has led the biologists to issue the appalling statement that ninety percent of evolution occurred before these invertebrates put in their appearance. I cannot but believe that such a pronouncement is really an effort on the part of the biologists to attract attention.

Your table shows that the Ordovician and Silurian periods followed the Cambrian. In the Silurian the trilobites are distinctly on the decline. Here appears the first air-breathing animal, a scorpion. The Ordovician and Silurian periods were molluscoid in their life forms —not particularly interesting. The Devonian Period was more prophetic. Vertebrates appear—fish, lots of them. And Yale University has a single Devonian footprint— the loneliest footprint in the world. The Pennsylvanian was the coal age. About the swamps of those days slithered amphibians. It was no great change from the amphibian to the mammal. A mammal is a warm-

A GEOLOGIC TABLE
(To be read from bottom to top for chronology)

ERA	PERIODS	LIFE CHARACTER
	Recent	
	Pleistocene	Rise of mammals.
Cenozoic	Pliocene	
	Miocene	Man is pretty well along by
	Oligocene	the Pliocene.
	Eocene	
Mesozoic	Cretaceous	Great variety of reptiles— the dinosaurs. Reptiles lead to birds. Beginnings of modern plants.
	Jurassic	
	Triassic	
	Permian	Amphibians lead to reptiles.
	Pennsylvanian	Amphibians appear. Many insects.
Paleozoic	Mississippian	These are the coal periods.
	Devonian	Fish as first vertebrates.
	Silurian	
	Ordovician	Trilobites, mollusca, corals.
	Cambrian	
Proterozic		Metamorphic rocks containing free carbon and lime elements.
Archaeozoic		Most ancient rocks. No evidence of life.

(The sedimentary rocks begin generally with the Paleozoic. The rocks of the Mesozoic are less indurated sedimentaries.)

blooded animal with hair on its body, which bears its young alive and suckles it at the breast. Don't worry that the whale has no hair, and that there is a mammal that lays eggs. Nature can be most unscientific.

Probably the succeeding Permian Period of glaciation gave the mammals their warm blood. From then on evolution became more and more rapid. The Mesozoic Age was one of reptiles. Dinosaurs ran, hopped, swam, and flew about the landscape. How by even the agencies of selection and mutation these beasts could have adapted themselves in so short a time to such varying habits, it is difficult to say. Fortunately their brains did not keep up with their bulk. By this negligence they created their own doom. The Cenozoic Age was one of mammals. Most of the physical features that characterize man probably were set by the end of the Miocene.

This is all to show that environmental influences have been at work these many eons. Since we started as a primordial protoplasm and progressed to our present twenty-six trillion cells we have been subjected continuously to the same kind of influences. Divergent and convergent evolution are nothing new. The principles of evolution are fossilized in stone and as such are more definite than when witnessed in our complex living world. The principles of evolution and environmentalism are best illustrated in geology.

Let us take, for example, these questions of divergent and convergent evolution. Again and again in the geologic past we see molluscs become separated from the main stream of progress. Isolated in some inland sea, it comes about that the isolated branch of the family evolves in a manner divergent from the main group. There is no reasonable probability that the two evolutions should be the same. Also, the isolated group probably has less stimulation to change (that is, is put through fewer environmental screens) and, therefore, crystallized the characters of the ancestor common to the two groups. The character of the Boers in Cloete's "The Turning Wheel" is an example of divergence from the main Dutch stock. Or take convergent evolution. The shark (a primitive fish), the Ichthyosaur (a Mesozoic swimming reptile) and the dolphin (a modern swimming mammal) all looked alike. The people of the Nile, of the Euphrates, and of the Ganges, for no common reason, all took to agriculture, another example of convergent social evolution.

More than merely elucidating principles of evolution, a study of the geologic past has the advantage of allowing one to study a period of longer duration than the present. Also, there were in those days no humanitarian instincts, no doctors to save the unfit, by which men might be saved from doom by changes of geographical environment.

In the Pliocene Period, something over a million years ago, some hairy anthropoid precursor of the true man roamed a rather pleasant forest in Central Asia, climbing trees as he saw need, though food was plentiful and beasts of prey do not usually climb trees. This squat, semi-erect individual probably thought that he was the acme of something. But he was just a beginning. Why do we place him in Central Asia? Because we know that the ripple farthest from where the pebble was dropped in the water is the oldest. From Asia as a center have come waves of migrations, and we find some of the oldest types on the extremities of the Eurasian continent. One early migration, for example, is evidenced in the ancient physical types of the English Celts, the Bretons of Finisterre and the peninsular Galicians of Iberia. So Roy Chapman Andrews hied himself to Central Asia to find the earliest skull and came back with a dinosaur egg. Dramatic, but, after all, disappointing.

The most primitive man we have so far discovered is less than a million years old.* His burial site (Java) is surrounded with the bones of twenty-six kinds of Pliocene animals. We are not yet certain who ate whom. This gentleman was no orang-outang but a human. Dentists know. Though called *Pithecanthropus erectus,* he stood not completely erect. He probably had a huge, ugly jaw, a short neck, and long arms. His skull, with less edible meat on it than his other bones, is the only part remaining to us. As a result of Dutch imperialism, it rests in Amsterdam.

By the comparatively recent date of 50,000 years ago,

---

* It may be that the Pekin or the Piltdown man is actually older than the Java man but they are less primitive. The question is yet to be settled.

there were many even more human specimens who had themselves conveniently buried in Europe. These people were of the Old Stone Age. No better book about them has been written than that by Osborn, called "Men of the Old Stone Age." These were men of open moorlands because once the forests in Central Asia had disappeared, and man was forced to live in the open, he was reluctant to return to the tree lands. Primitives are slow to change their environment. On the plains, with hands free for grasping, the men lived as groups. No longer did they scatter among the trees when frightened. They gathered rather in herds with the old patriarch as a governor. One tended the fire, some stood guard, some hunted for the group; women went to the stream for water. Man was discovering social organization and the division of labor.

About one half million years ago the lands of Europe began to chill. Each winter a little more snow fell in Scandinavia than melted in summer. No element of man's environment is more inconstant than weather. From day to day the weather changes and it is hardly to be expected that the average weather of one year will be that of the next. Average weather is called climate, and climate changes, but we think we know it does not always change in one direction. Rather it goes to one extreme and back to the other, like swings of a pendulum. Some swings seem only a dozen years in length. Some are hundreds of centuries long. The average climate of geologic periods was apparently considerably warmer than the climate of historical periods and yet a score of times in geologic history the pendulum has swung to colder weather when glaciers formed. The last glacier period—there have been almost a score of them—was what we call the Great Ice Age. It is not yet over but the pendulum is swinging back. The world is probably getting warmer.

What causes these ages of ice? Perhaps they are the result of a number of factors. This much seems to be true. What apparently controls activity of the atmosphere and creates storms is the irregularity of energy given out by the sun. When there is great volcanic activity on the sun (such volcanoes appear to us as sun spots) there is always great change and usually great storminess in our local weather. Now, snow comes from storms at low temperatures. All that is necessary to form a glacier is to have enough snow in one place, for a glacier is merely a body of ice that moves under its own weight. Therefore, glaciers are found near storm centers and particularly where the land is chilled at high elevations.

Glaciers are common in mountains, but in the Ice Age they covered huge areas in North America and Eurasia, which were known as continental ice sheets. The ice sheet which was most important to history is the Eurasian sheet. It covered the Scandinavian countries and the British Isles. It reached down into Germany (see map), spread over northern Russia and northwestern Siberia. Eastern Siberia was the coldest part of Eurasia, yet it was without ice sheets. Why? Because eastern Siberia had little precipitation, not enough snow.

Great piles of snow turned to ice. The weight of the ice at the center of the mass caused the glacier to move outwards in all directions. Thus the ice, as thick as mountains are high, crept over half a continent. Great arms of ice filled the valleys, and the glacier covered the hills. Freezing on to soil and loose rock, the glacier, shod with sharp tools, ground down the hills and gouged out the valleys. From the region of the center, soil and loose rock were carried away to be cast aside in moraines near the margins of the area to which the ice extended. All this is physical geography.

In the region where the glacier originated it was, of course, cold and stormy. So much ice accumulated that the glacier thrust itself into climates which were really not frigid. Finally a stage was reached where the warmth melted the ice as rapidly as the ice came on. Nor was the climate within the period of the ice duration always the same. At times of greater cold and snow the ice advanced far; at other times the edge of the ice retreated. There were within the Great Ice Age four chief advances of the ice.

Environment ordinarily does little in developing new human characters and attributes under normal conditions. Environments are usually looked upon as passive and merely limiting influences. But when the environment changes, and dramatically, it becomes an active

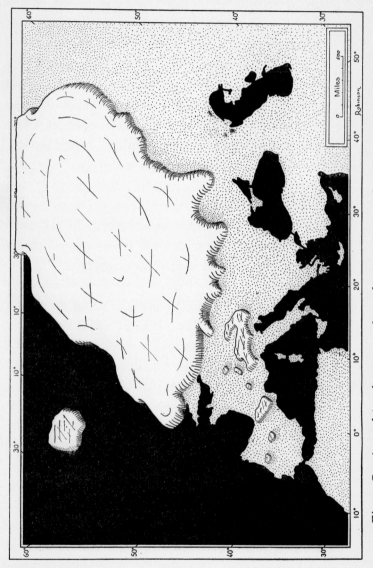

Fig. 4. Continental ice sheets spread out from a center and cover mountain and sea. It is curious how exactly this covers the war zone today. Grant us, Oh Lord, a change of climate.

agent. Remember that in Europe there were primitive
men roaming the forests before the ice first advanced.
The chilling of the air by the change in climate and
the actual refrigeration due to the advancing ice must
have challenged man to fight for his existence. The
weaker men died off. Those who lived made greater
use of fire, sought shelter in caves and provided themselves with fur garments. The glacier forced man to a
greater use of his intelligence and by the process of
selection physically improved the race. Ice actually
forced the commencement of the higher mind of art
and industry. Moreover, it caused selective migrations.
Perhaps the most intelligent men moved south. The
others perished or existed precariously by their wits.
Between the advances of the ice were periods of ice
retreat, known as the interglacial periods. Each time
the ice retreated northward, the primitive hunters followed. Here is a table which indicates the duration
of the interglacial periods. Historically this table should
be read from the bottom up. Of course, the figures of
years are not accurate; the geologist has various ways of
measuring time but he cannot be so exact. See table,
page 73.

We have said that during geologic periods the shapes
of continents were not constant. During this half-mil-
lion years of the ice age there were important coastline
changes, especially about the Mediterranean Sea. Land
rises and sinks easily. The weight of the ice alone was
sufficient to cause it to sink. In the first interglacial

period, land in the area of the Mediterranean Sea rose
as much as 300 feet. Land bridges between Africa and
Europe were formed at Gibraltar and from Italy to
Africa by way of the island of Sicily. Great hairy ele-
phants as well as other beasts invaded Europe from
Africa over these bridges. Some of the time the British
Islands were connected with the mainland. There was
no Baltic Sea.

	LENGTH OF EACH PERIOD	SUM OF ALL PERIODS
Postglacial Stage		
Paleolithic man, particularly the Cro-Magnon man	25,000 yrs.	25,000 yrs.
Fourth Glacial Period		
Neanderthal man	25,000	50,000
3rd Interglacial Period		
Early Paleolithic man	100,000	150,000
Third Glacial Period	25,000	175,000
2nd Interglacial Period		
Heidelberg man	200,000	375,000
Second Glacial Period	25,000	400,000
1st Interglacial Period		
Pithecanthropus or Java man	75,000	475,000
First Glacial Period	25,000	500,000

With each advance of the ice the character of the
animals changed. The second interglacial period had
the giant deer, bison, cattle, horse, boar, wolf, fox and
bear. Following this the third period had the southern
mammoth, the elephant, rhinoceros, hippopotamus,
lions and saber-tooth tigers. Every new animal was a

challenge to man, testing and tempering the steel of his intelligence.

Lull, my favorite evolutionist, says, "Changing environmental conditions stimulate the sluggish evolution-

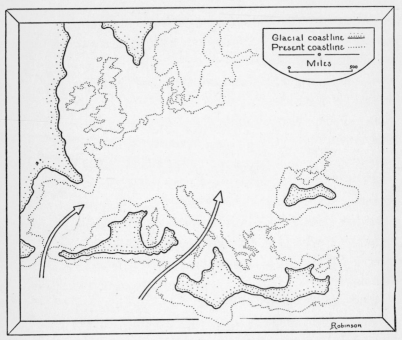

Glacial coastline ....
Present coastline ....
0
Miles
0   500

Robinson

Fig. 5. In interglacial periods there were land bridges between Europe and Africa permitting migrations of man and beast. The dotted lines show Europe's contour today.

ary stream to quickened movement." In terms of the total history of mankind the thrusts of the ice created exceedingly rapid changes of environment. More than that, their effect upon the evolution of man was decisive and dramatic. It was as if a series of selective screens sifted out the unfit. Surely man was receiving now his mental superiority to the other animals. Europe was well populated before the ice, if we may judge by the stratigraphic location of the bones and artifacts, and the inhabitants were forced to deal with a new climate, one not too warm and certainly one with an increased storminess. New plants of an arctic nature supplied food. The moors which replaced the woods were inhabited by fierce beasts entirely new to the human hunter. Food, shelter, clothing, and defense in their new aspects all called for an increased ingenuity if men were to continue to exist.

In the third interglacial period came the immediate forerunner of true man. This physical type, being our own, has been naïvely named by ourselves *Homosapiens*—the wise man. One group, the Cro-Magnons, came to Europe out of the southeast and the other, a negroid type called Grimaldi, walked over from Africa by those convenient land bridges.

These men in time developed the Neolithic or New Stone Age. They were the first to develop to any appreciable extent the environmental resources to their uses. We have from them polished and refined stone weapons and tools, and also the bow and arrow, which permitted man to kill without coming in contact with the beast.*

---

* "The Story of Ab" by Stanley Waterloo tells interestingly of this period. Good for ages eight to eighty.

On the walls of their caves these men drew, as did
the early American Indians, the pictures of the animals
they hunted. The drawings were scratched in the stone
and crudely colored. The red, black, brown, white and
yellow pigments have survived to this day in certain
caves in Spain. One of the drawings, a spirited interpretation of a bison chase, is done in four colors. At
this time men also began to carve soft stone and ivory
into rounded shapes, little grotesques of women and
animals. In one cave there were found sea-shells, pierced
as if to be strung in ornaments. Men began to treat
their own bodies with greater respect, and probably
painted their skins for much the same reasons that we
wear bright colors. Their dead were buried with weapons, and food was placed near the great, unclasped
hands.

It is interesting that men alone, of all the animals,
had a sense of art. These first true men were not only
concerned with feeding, sleeping, defending themselves and reproducing their kind, but they also turned
to art to express their ideas about their world. They
attempted to beautify themselves and their surroundings. Early art was very closely associated with the
idea of magic. A belief in magic is characteristic of
most primitive people even today. The image of an
animal or person is often thought to give the painter
magic power over the object pictured. Some primitive
people today will refuse to give their names to a
stranger lest by so doing they give themselves into the

power of that stranger. Thus the many drawings on the walls of the prehistoric caves are thought to be early evidence of man's attempt to gain extraordinary power over his world. By the drawings on the walls of his cave and on his weapons he hoped to be able to kill the animals he represented.

Early man was, then, almost wholly a creature of his environment. In spite of the frigid glacial climate, in some favored place the most healthy and intelligent men continued to exist. Again and again that puny creature, Man, whose hope of survival lay in his cleverness, walking on two legs, crept stealthily forth into the world he meant to conquer. In a few feeble ways he learned to make his environment serve him. Occasionally he could defend himself from the ravenous beasts. He sought out the regions which served him with the surest food. In some moment of tremendous excitement he discovered how to make fire. While the earth was plowed with ice, while mountains gradually sank under the sea, and new lands encrusted with shells emerged, Man, standing upright on some remote beach, looked about with bright eyes, and wondered how he might survive.

What this glacial period proves as most important but which are frequently overlooked, are facts leading to a defeat of the anti-evolutionists.* The fundamental-

* The struggle with the animal for survival is not entirely a thing of the past. In 1922 in India, 20,090 persons were killed by snakes, 1,613 by tigers, 509 by leopards, 9 by hyaenas, 90 by pigs, 225 by crocodiles, by other animals 207, a total of over

ist says "Behold the Greek!" He had an excellent physique, and has there been better reasoning than Plato's or more crystal rationalizing than Euclid's? In other words, in the last 2500 years we have not greatly evolved. An answer is that the human being does not greatly change except as his environment changes. In the mere 2500 years that have passed since the day of the Greek there has been little perceptible physical or mental evolution. Angell offers the opinion that there has been no mental evolution since the beginning of history. This is probably true but it is hardly optimistic. Yet these last millenniums have been the period of civilization, invention for safety and comfort, medical science and relative humanity. All the agents of civilization work together for a defeat of evolution by selection. Appendectomies, air-conditioned houses, conquest of the animal world, and devices of safety have all but negated natural selection.

By the devious road of this chapter where have we arrived? We have, it is hoped, absorbed as if by osmosis the concept that the great changes in environment in the geologic past played a great part in evolution. Nor have those changes ceased. We do not observe their action for life is so short and art and evolution so long that as humans we lack micrometers sufficiently fine by which to measure such slow progress.

23,353. Men killed 58,370 snakes and 23,268 other animals. Man does better in his battle against animals than autos. R. S. Lull, "The Ways of Life," 1925, p. 74.

Chapter Five

A THESIS OF

GEOGRAPHY

WHETHER OR NOT MAN'S FIRST INTELLIGENCE CAN BE ascribed to mutations or to the tests which the ice thrusts created, man by the end of the glacial period had definitely a clever brain, not a mere nerve control which moved his body and allowed him to garner his food. More than that, he stood erect, leaving two arms free, and he had the easily opposable thumb. How much of civilization is ascribable to this thumb, which by touching the other finger tips permits man to hold objects, can only be guessed. But man had come through the experience of the relentless glacial period triumphant. He had conquered the world. We can think of him as standing at the entrance of his cave, facing the rising sun, and giving vent to a half howl and half laugh of victory. Had he realized the foibles and furies of his trillions of descendants his laugh might well have become a sardonic groan.

Our hairy hero already had achieved an inventive, a creative, and a mystic mind. But as yet he had hardly more of a culture than the bear that collects food and goes to sleep in a cave. True, man was using stone, wood, fire and hides in a superior manner. The first stone used was as a fist hammer. The hammer placed on the end of a stick became an ax and was much more effective. Fire for warmth and cooking was an important aspect of the culture. Hides were dressed with simple scrapers and used for clothing. Stones themselves were sharpened by chipping and were polished, and it is that patient polishing of stone tools which marks the beginning of the New Stone Age, or Neolithic, as distinguished from the Old Stone Age or Paleolithic. If in these early days man did not greatly alter his environment, the environment did not develop varying habits of life. Man was a wanderer, not fixed to one place long enough to be deeply impressed by environment. The restless never take on color from the landscape. It is this tint of place that represents environmentalism, local color, if you will.

In this period of polished stone implements man was inventing and by such invention was overcoming the obstacle of habit. He went further and began adapting natural resources to his purpose. Now geographic processes develop the reciprocal relationship, the part wherein man affects his environment. One invention particularly was revolutionary, the bow and stone-tipped arrow. Its inventor was a medicine man, an Edison, a Steinmetz.

Also, in this period came the domestication of animals. All men love the young offspring of humans or of beasts. The young of the beasts were kept after the mothers had been killed off. Reared together, the man-child and the puppy, calf or colt formed partnerships. Man offered protection and, in return, took milk, hunting, and burden-bearing services from the beasts.

But the most significant, new relationship between man and his milieu in these pre-historic days was agriculture. It was significant not only because of the intelligence it implied but because of its profound influence. Somewhere in the Near East man is believed first to have discovered that grain could be raised from seed. He had been wont to collect the wild grain kernels for food. We can imagine lowly ancestors cautiously entering a grain prairie to collect seeds in baskets or hide pokes. They returned to the tribal retreat to feed the young or very old. Perhaps the grain was parched over a fire. Some was accidentally spilled on ground made fertile by wood ashes. And then a superman, pondering upon the dense stand of grain about last year's camping ground, saw the truth. Swinging an ax for authority, he forced his improvident people to save part of their food for planting. Equally a man of magic was the hero who forced his people to select the best seeds and so improved the crop. The domestication of plants is older than history. Barley, wheat, millet, beans, peas, flax and many fruits were cultivated and improved before history was recorded.

The development of tillage culture was one of the great revolutions of history. Nothing more changed man's way of living, unless it was the development of machinery in the nineteenth century. It was the first great conquest of nature, far more important than the use of stone or the herding of animals. The native vegetation of river plains gave way to cultivated, man-chosen plants. Forests were cleared for fields. In time, rivers were turned aside to irrigate the land. With the coming of agriculture, man forced his desires upon the countryside. He looked upon a cultural landscape rather than a wild one. The land became *his* land. He was learning how to adapt the earth's surface to his needs, using the earth itself as a material of life. The period when the native surroundings determined man's welfare was passing. Man began to see that he could dominate the landscape and so determine his own comfort.

The actual meaning of this new geographic relationship between man and earth is important. Instead of continuing his life as a wanderer, a gatherer of such foods as he might find, he became fixed in one place.

In that place he changed the surroundings to suit his needs. At the same time, he himself had to meet the changes that came with living in a fixed environment. When men wandered about, eating such food as they found ready to be consumed, no great numbers herded together. A tribe in the collectional stage of culture can support no greater numbers than can be fed upon the food of the least productive season, winter. But the agriculturalist had a storehouse in which he kept the surplus of food from summer until winter. This allowed a larger number of people to live in a given area. Living close together, men were called upon to adjust themselves to the needs and wants of their fellows. The community was established.

Men who remain fixed, as in a community, are called sedentaries. Men who have no fixed abode, who wander constantly as do the herders on the plains searching for greener grass for their beasts, are called nomads. The fixed abode of the sedentary encourages more than the building of storehouses for surplus food and tools. In a sense, sedentaries also develop a storehouse of ideas. From past experiences of one generation knowledge may be passed on to the next generation living in that same environment. Progress is built, in part, on a certain sameness of experience which only long residence in one place by a community group can bring about. We, therefore, find that with the introduction of agriculture and the growth of the community, culture progressed in mighty strides.

A first condition of a community development is a means of communication. Spoken communication is language. How the first guttural utterings of savages came to have meanings we can only guess. Once having developed agriculture, which fixed numbers of men together, we may be sure that language advanced rapidly.

Equally fundamental to a group-life are certain regulations of inter-relationship. There must be some kind of law. Even in the cruder groups of the early Paleolithic Age there was leadership. The Old Man of the family group was the leader. It is believed that he drove out of the family group the younger men as they came to be his rivals. Law, then, began with the will of the strongest or wisest man of the group. As many families came to live together in an agricultural community, there probably developed a council of the wise or strong.

It must soon have become apparent also that an advantage could be gained from a division of labor. Certain men or women came to work in the fields. One tended the cattle. Another plowed. Others reaped in season. Certain individuals were professional soldiers who stood guard. Pottery workers and weapon makers were those who proved themselves most skillful in these arts. The beginning of civilization might well be called the beginning of specialization.

It is not difficult to see how community life brings about commerce. One man tills the soil and tends the animals. Another makes pottery or weapons. Within the group trading must begin when specialization occurs. Trading increases specialization, and specialization increases efficiency. Soon one community becomes noted for the fine bows and arrows it produces. This group may have opened trade with a community noted for the durability of its pottery.

Few regions in the world have all the resources needed for an advanced civilization. One region may lack clothing materials; another lacks wood for the building of ships; while yet another lacks metals for tools and utensils. Except for man's intelligence and initiative, civilizations would have remained local affairs, limited by what nature locally provided. But the mind of man has always been characterized by a will to adventure, to go beyond the immediate confines of his vision. In some undetermined period before history began, savage man sought the advantages of resources found in other regions. He desired, as he does today, to get for himself the best his world had to offer.

It is important, of course, that people lacking certain materials should obtain them through commerce. But perhaps it is more important still that each culture receive new ideas from other regions. New ideas are stimulating, and they mean progress. The spread of ideas is slow but it is made more rapid by commerce. Traders and peddlers took with them ideas as surely as they carried commodities in their packs. "Ideas are light baggage." Therefore, progress in civilization can frequently be measured by the commercial contacts which a people had. The history of commerce is one way of describing the breakdown of provincialism.

Man's mind, characterized by the will to adventure in unknown physical worlds, is characterized also by the will to explore unknown areas of ideas. When man had the leisure time that came with specialization and the assurance of food and shelter, he turned to invention. At first he used this leisure almost exclusively to invent things which combined to make his life more comfortable and safe. It was during this early period that weaving was begun. Fibers from the flax plant, from wool and even from bark were twisted into thread by rubbing against the thigh. Next a spindle was attached to the fibers and the weight spun about. The weaving of wattles (walls made of woven reeds) was partly an improved shelter construction. Some of the early man-made shelters were holes in the ground protected by wicker work. The house above the ground followed.

For defense man raised houses upon sticks or piles. A great settlement of early houses was set on piles above water. The "lake dwellers'" houses were first discovered in a very dry winter nearly a hundred years ago when the water level of a Swiss lake sank low enough to reveal the foundations half buried in the peat-like bottom of the lake. The peat had preserved the remains. A careful study of these interesting remnants of the past showed that the people who lived in these houses were of the Neolithic Age. Utensils and ornaments were found, food and pieces of clothing and nets which these savage men had cast for fishes. In one settlement there were about fifty houses set on stilts and having walks which allowed the people to go above the water from house to house.*

During the period of early agriculture, pottery was much improved. The tilling of clay fields and the making of pottery have always gone together. The widespread use of pottery meant that men could live some distance from the source of water. More than this, people now cooked their food in vessels. Cooking no longer meant mere roasting.

It was thousands of years after the first use of wood, stone and bone for tools that men began to use metal. About 6,000 years or more ago the Neolithic peoples began to use copper. One reason that copper was probably the first metal used is because it is attractively colored and is heavier than stone. Sometimes copper is found in a pure state. More often it comes as an ore mixed with other elements. Such ore would have to be smelted to remove the copper mineral. This was not an easy process and men showed a great advance when they were able to figure out the necessary steps. The men who stood at the first forges and brought forth the melted ore must have seemed to be strange and perhaps terrible wizards. When tin was added to copper and a

* In Venezuela, Borneo and elsewhere we still have pile dwellings.

fused metal which we call bronze was made, man had forged for himself a really superior metal. Bronze is harder than either tin or copper and can therefore hold a sharper cutting edge. The use of bronze was so important to man that we give its name to a stage of culture; the Bronze Age. The Bronze Age extended into the historical period, but so for that matter did the Neolithic culture. Both of these Ages, we must remember, are stages of cultural development, not periods of time.

The peoples at the eastern end of the Mediterranean seem to have been the first to use bronze. An interesting thing about the use of bronze is that people must have had to travel great distances to get the tin which was used in the making of this metal. Thus the use of bronze meant that an early commerce was carried on between the eastern Mediterranean and such far-distant places of tin deposits as those perhaps of Malaya, Spain, Central Europe, or even the British Isles.

By 4000 B.C. the two great nurseries of civilization had come to be the valleys of the Nile and Euphrates Rivers. It was in Egypt and Mesopotamia that Neolithic men had found the surest food supply for themselves and their beasts, and the materials at hand for the construction of houses. This security encouraged a definite abandonment of the nomadic life. Cultivation in these protected areas and on the Island of Crete at the eastern end of the Mediterranean, swiftly outdistanced the developments of cultures in less favorable areas and amongst people still wandering in search of food. Egypt and Mesopotamia probably saw the earliest dense populations of men tilling the earth on a large scale. These peoples were trading with other regions and were living under social laws and regulations while men of Europe were still in the early Neolithic stages of culture. It was in these regions that men first attempted to make definite records for future generations to decipher.

If men became fixed in place, if generation after generation of men tilled the same soil and watched for the return of the same harvests, then it is no startling conclusion that the variations in soil, climate and crops began by their very monotony to create cultures deeply colored by the peculiarities of place. Regional geography begins when peoples become fixed. Then the kaleidoscope of cultures takes on contrasted hues. When man came to be stationary in order to profit by his adaptation of the local resources, the landscape had an opportunity to begin the slow but persistent effect upon man.

It was at this stage of history that provincialisms came into being. Geography is essentially a study of provincial contrasts. No contrasts—no geography. Once men became sedentaries the contrasted elements of landscape insidiously and almost imperceptibly began their work. Semple says that man has been noisy about his conquest of nature, yet nature, though quiet, has been most effective in changing the life of man. The struggle is not unlike the race between the hare and tortoise, with man as the hare, and nature as the tortoise.

How many of these provincial differences are the result of physical circumstances and how many due to leadership of differing historical trend it is impossible to say. May I again use the device of the cube with the inevitable X, Y and Z? Consider X as the cultural inheritance, Y the effect of physical environment and Z the importance of leadership, invention or what you will.

In the very early stages of a group's development physical circumstance stamped the cultural fact or event with its character. Later inventiveness played a greater and greater part in provincial quality. Cultural inheritance, of course, accumulated strength with the centuries. Hence the more modern the scene, the less there is of the environmental factor in culture and the greater the importance of the work of man.

A province is any portion of the earth with somewhat uniform physical characteristics and natural resources, differing from adjacent regions, which results in a common economy and a group consciousness among the local inhabitants. How uniform shall be the resources and economy within the region and how well defined the group consciousness, it is difficult to say. One geographer can scarcely mark off the world map into provincialisms in a manner satisfactory to any other geographer. Seacoasts, mountain ranges and climatic boundaries all fail in a world-wide application. Some provinces have great personality, while others are hardly susceptible to any limitation.

And so we must leave off treating man without locale. We have not only tied him to the earth but we have fixed one group of men in one pocket, a river valley, and another group perhaps on some plateau with few resources but stimulating climate. Groups of men now begin to have separate histories. To study these histories we must look to the character of our varied earth, to the fertilities of the soil, to the fluctuating weathers and to the distribution of land and water.

The roots of history run deep into the ground. The ground with its infinite variety has produced kaleidoscopic culture. Some elements of this infinite variety are simple. A mountain barrier is an obvious and tangible thing. Seas are seas and to the eye much alike. It is the interactions of the elements of physical circumstance which create complexity. Take the sum totals of geographic position, isolation or accessibility, the numerous details of topography, soils and climate—and one can expect multitudinous variety. It is little wonder that the historian, though he may acknowledge the importance of geography in history, hesitates to use the principle of relationship. To analyze elements of landscape and climate and weigh their functions calls for a special training. Therefore, it is more the fault of the geographer than the historian that geography in history has been so much ignored. Yet the chief joy in social history is the running to earth, to the very soil, the facts of history. The variety makes the adventure more exciting. It is the unexpected in journeying through "My Great, Wide Beautiful World" which keeps one on the go.

History then is no longer rote learning of a sequence of facts but a study to stimulate and excite. Here is a painted desert; there are old, low mountains, forested in monotonous green. Here are endless miles of yellow wheat; there is hill country, barren except for gray-green patches of olive trees. Each forces a different manner of earning a living and a different manner of thinking. The raiding nomad, living from his flocks or from booty, was as much a product of his wind-swept plains as was the Provençal troubadour the result of his sunny hills. Geography seems to have destined that London should be a port to welcome ships from the ends of the earth. Likewise there is geographical and historical reason for coal mining and steel making in the Saar valley.

Such facts seem reasonable and orderly. The details are a part of the scheme of things. But there are larger controls which are not so obvious. One has to do with the arrangement of land and water. A most fundamental fact in human history is that one-fourth of the earth's surface is land and that something like one-fifth of the land is practically uninhabitable. Moreover, the land areas lie scattered over the whole globe much as hot solder spatters on the floor.

The largest land mass is Eurasia. India is a peninsular extension, and western Europe a series of peninsulas. Look at the map. The continents are lifted from the globe and laid on a plane. The map shows Africa, North America and South America as appen-

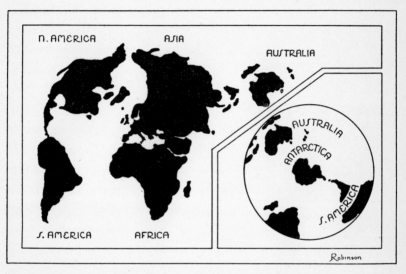

Fig. 6. This chart shows how Eurasia is the central land mass and all the rest appendages or islands. The inset shows how Australia and South America are near to each other. Here was the one-time land bridge that permitted the migration of the marsupials.

dages from the central mass. Once Australia was connected through Antarctica with South America. We believe the present shallows connecting the continents were dry land because both continents have examples of those extraordinary animals that carry their young in a pocket. The Australian marsupial is the kangaroo and the American marsupial is the opossum. It does not seem as if the Creator would have bothered to do the same special thing twice. The two must have had a common ancestor that migrated via a warmer Antarctica. If it is true that human life began in Central Asia, then we can rightly think of remote land areas as having the most primitive societies, at least before the days of ocean sailing. Tierra del Fuego, lying off the southern tip of South America, was before 1492 the most remote of lands. The miserable aborigines of that land were certainly primitive when discovered by the white man. If men reached the remoter continents by land bridges or by crossing narrow straits, bridges and straits are among the most interesting places to study.

Historically speaking, I suppose there is no more important piece of sand in the world than the isthmus of Suez. This isthmus more or less coincided in ancient times with the Land of Goshen. Goshen formed a gateway to Egypt, the only weakness in the natural fortifications which gave that country its isolation. Through the Land of Goshen the Arabian Hyksos introduced the horse into Egyptian culture. Their invasion indicated the possibility of a return passage of the isthmus by which the Egyptian charioteers could spread terror through Palestine and Syria and found an empire. There were also, of course, the Israelite passages of the isthmus. To appreciate the cultural significance of all this, read James Breasted's "The Dawn of Conscience." The extent to which the Egyptian scriptures influenced

THE
ISTHMUS of SUEZ
Each section on the arrow
represents about 1000 mi.
Scale on the small map
0   100
Miles

Robinson—

Fig. 7. Think what history would have been had there been no deposit of sand named Suez!

the Hebrew shows the vast importance of this land connection.

If the isthmus was a great passageway for men and ideas, it was of even greater significance as a barrier to sea travel. The sixth century B.C. flourished with almost equal brilliance in Greece and in India. Yet these two civilizations were quite remote by land and completely without sea communication. What might have been their history had there been no Isthmus of Suez? So divergent are the traditions of the East and the West, and so fixed are they by the centuries that in spite of the present canal it seems doubtful the two should ever coincide.

This is but a note upon one strip of sand. What would history have been had the Hellespont been a land bridge, the Pillars of Hercules a barrier to sea travel, or had there been no Isthmus of Panama? Had the Aleutian Islands been continuous land might not the Americas have been open to the medieval Mongols?

The great land bodies that lie curled around the globe have wrinkles and fractured blocks. These are mountains. The study of their origin is geology. Their distribution has reason. Often in parallel ridges, elsewhere in clusters, there lie between them valleys, passes, saddles and corridors. One hardly need point out the importance of the barriers. The Pyrenees separate Spain and France. So important are mountains as barriers that the passes have been jammed throughout the centuries by the pageants of history. Between the Vosges Moun-

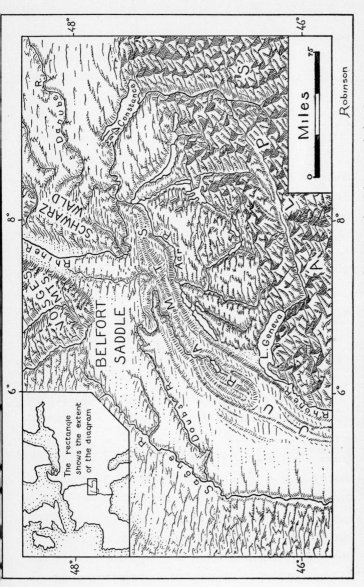

Fig. 8. How the Belfort Saddle forms a way between the Rhine and the Saone systems.

tains and the Jura lies the Belfort Saddle. Caesar first
came into Gaul to help hold that pass against the
Germanii. During the World War the Italians again
came to brace the eastern gates against the Germans.

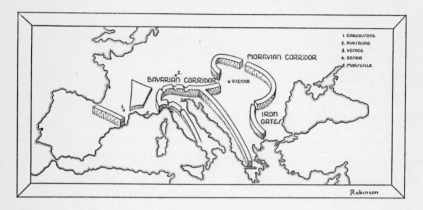

Fig. 9. Carcassone, Augsburg, Venice, Genoa and Marseille
are some of the pass cities or gate cities of Europe. If converging arrows are drawn through the Bavarian, Moravian
and Iron Gates corridors the situation of Vienna is explained.

The above map shows the skeleton ranges of Europe
upon which the flesh (plains) is hung. To illustrate
the importance of the road between the mountains
draw inward three arrows converging upon each other,
one through the Moravian corridor, the Bavarian corridor and the Iron Gates of the Danube. Where these
converge you find Vienna. The passages, saddles and
corridors explain such cities as Cologne, Carcassonne
and Langres. Augsburg, Innsbruck and Venice lie

along a trans-Alpine route. Genoa is a port but also a pass city. Marseilles guards the Rhone route. Lyon is at a junction of the ways.

Asia is replete with such examples. There are Samarkand and Kashgar at the bases of the pass of the Pamirs. There is one pass between the Iran Plateau and the Indian Plain. This is the Khyber Pass through which countless hordes of soldiers, beasts and peddlers have passed. It would take a Walt Whitman to give such a list its true romantic cadence: foot travelers, donkeys, camels, elephants, caravans, armies, motor cars and tanks.*

These corridors are the ruts of the world, be they land routes or water passages. Along them has flowed the freight of the centuries and ideas as well. The ruts are important in both commercial geography and in the history of ideas for they have given direction to the diffusion of cultures. This brings me to an important point, which is that every cargo ship that drops anchor in a quiet harbor, every caravan that comes to rest in a caravansery brings with it an invisible cargo of ideas. Along the freight routes flowed wheat, salt and amber; ivory, apes and peacocks. The wheat and salt are consumed. The amber goes to a girl of passing fancy. The ivory, apes and peacocks become Biblical poetry. But the ideas flowing over these routes are not all lost. Greek art concepts flowed through the Khyber Pass, along the Ganges rut, through the Burma-Yunnan

* A fine "pass" book is J. E. Tyler's, "The Alpine Passes."

route and live in the monasteries of southern China today. The heresy of municipal freedom was transported
by peddlers through the passes of the Alps from the

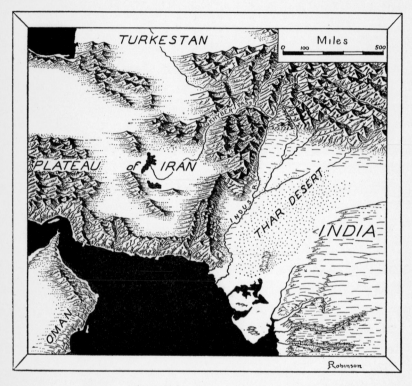

Fig. 10. The Khyber Pass is the one way to and from India
on the west.

Lombard cities to the feudal towns of the Rhine.
Cologne was an early free city of the north. So many
ideas from the enlightened Mediterranean passed with
the freight up the Rhone Valley following the Dark

Ages that that valley is known as the Way of Light.*

A beautiful example of ideas in camel bags is found in the Lob Desert along the silk route from Cathay. The Lob Desert lies in Central Asia. There in burial tombs are conventional Chinese cloud scrolls on silk. But over the scrolls are Greek designs. Here caravans met and ideas were exchanged. Or again, there was a remarkable route which led from the Mediterranean, up the Nile to the cataracts, and thence overland through Ethiopia to the Indian Ocean. And, to the geographer's delight, there is a temple in Ethiopia combining Greek and Indian art.

When the history of the diffusion of ideas is written, it will largely resemble a geography. And what a grand book it will be! How great a joy it would have been to have owned a villa overlooking the Straits of Messina, there to consider the invisible freights of the ships daring Scylla and Charybdis to bring grain to the ports of Rome. It would be an education in modern international affairs to know all that has passed along the Rome-Berlin axis through the Brenner pass.

Thus we have before us the thesis of geography. Simply stated, it is that once man became fixed provincial cultures were evolved. The characters of these cultures depended in part upon the differences of natural endowment of the separate regions and, in part, upon the inventive contributions which groups of men or leaders

* See Griffith Taylor, "Environment and Nation." You will also want to know of his "Environment, Race and Migration."

of groups made. But hardly had provincialism fixed itself on men, guiding one people in this direction and yet another in that, when commerce began to equalize the differences in natural endowment, giving sea salt to the interior, and metals to the alluvial plain. Historical commercial geography is the basis for the history of diffusion of ideas.

Chapter Six

THE IMPORTANCE OF

ISOLATION

I<small>N ELEMENTARY GEOGRAPHY WE TEACH ABOUT SECTIONS</small> of the earth as if they were entirely distinct from each other. The customs of Holland, windmills, wooden shoes, brick houses, allegedly stolid farmers, are taught as if entirely and distinctively Dutch. As a matter of fact, windmills are Persian in origin, wooden shoes are characteristic of all northwestern Europe, the Babylonians first made bricks, and stolid characters are Neolithic holdovers. In advanced geography we break down this regional character. By the movements of history and commerce we show the realism of great interchange and that, as it says in "Saul," we are bound together in the bundle of life. Yet, to a greater or lesser extent, distinction of culture is a function of isolation. Without this factor we would have no contrasts, and the contrasts are the basis of geography. The early Netherlanders had no word for bog, because their landscape was *all* bog. Without isolation we would lack the divergent evolution which gives us our infinite variety. This chapter attempts to present isolation as a factor in provincialism.

One of the difficulties that confronts the historical environmentalist is that of separating the indigenous elements of culture from those elements which are the result of contacts with other lands, the result of diffusion by traders, or by invading armies. Egypt is a happy selection for the beginning of cultural history not only because of chronology but because its early culture is the most simple, the purest and the most nearly indigenous. So, as Miss Semple would say, let us set the stage for the Egyptian drama.

The Nile rises in equatorial Africa in a region of year-round rains. Its waters never fail the hundreds of miles of valley in the desert. But, there are certain tributaries that drain the highlands of Ethiopia. Ethiopia has copious summer water, and this surplus creates the famous floods. The Nile flows from jungle highlands across savanna and steppe. In the steppe area the river is incised in a gorge of sandstone. Occasional barriers of crystalline rock create cataracts and prohibit navi-

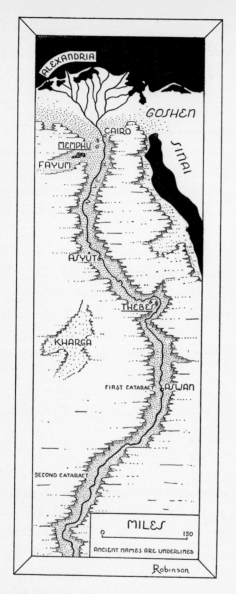

Fig. 11. In Egypt the physical conditions do not change, only the place names.

gation. Not far below the first cataract the river valley is walled by limestone. Limestone is easily soluble. Here the valley is more than a gorge. For 550 miles it is four to twelve miles in breadth. It is this strip which is Egypt—a mere pencil line on the map of Africa. So dramatic is the contrast between Egypt and the desert, so decisive the boundary, that one may stand with one foot in fertile Egypt and the other in the desert.

There are many names which through the centuries have meant Egypt. There are Khufer and Kafre, Thutmose III, and the bearded lady, Hatshepsut. Amenhotep III was the peacemaker. Ikhnaton was the great idealist. But these names are the product of Egypt. The one word which is basic, causal, in Egyptian history is Cheme. Cheme means "the black earth," and that is Egypt.

Not only was Egypt clearly defined from the desert without transition, the land of Cheme was isolated from the rest of the ancient world. No fact is more important in early Egyptian history than this isolation. The valley was flanked each side by uninhabitable desert. Since time immemorial there have been considerable populations to the South in the Sudan, anciently called Nubia, but there was during the first centuries little inter-communication. The steppe was broad and hot and the cataracts prevented river travel. One might expect the Nile travel to have continued on to the Medi-

terranean. But here again was a barrier. The very process of delta-making means the dissipation of waters
into numerous winding, shallow and uncertain channels which in flood time are obliterated. There was no
communication possible between the sea and the river.
The one "door" into Egypt was the Land of Goshen
described in the previous chapter. So Egypt stood alone,
self-contained, and of necessity its culture was essentially
indigenous.

Before 5000 B.C. strangers came into Egypt, bronze-
skinned men who were herders. They killed off some
aborigines and settled down. Even the environmentalist
shies from so sentimental a statement as "Nature points
the way," yet it is interesting how so many moistened
valleys, the Wei, the Yangste, the Ganges, the Euphrates
and the Nile, *did* point the way to agriculture. In any
case, these Stone Age herders were soon farming.
Cheme was destined to teach men to hoe. Still, after
those centuries, the almost naked *fellah* toils in his hot,
moist fields. Then as now, the chief concern of the
Egyptian government was agriculture. All during the
classical period Egypt was a great granary. Wheat and
barley flourished prodigiously in this soil fertilized
annually by a layer of silt from the flood. There were
vegetables, ground fruits and the all-important date.
There was no need to import food, little need to sell it.
Clothing came from the wool of the flocks that were
driven across the moist fields so that their hoofs might
press the seed into the ground. Linen was made from

flax. Housing was often four mud walls that cast a shadow over the enclosure. There were no roofs, for roofs retain heat, and rain in Egypt is almost unknown. In the walls of the valley was stone for the building of temples. Perhaps the peaceful isolation of Egypt provided labor which otherwise might have been spent in war. Copper, chiefly in the nearby Sinai Peninsula, led to the Chalcolithic Age. The Bronze Age called for the development of trade with some unknown and probably distant source of tin. The point to bring home is that Egyptian culture was based upon an adaptation of local resources and it was limited by those resources.

Man does not live by bread alone. A culture has political expressions and, when advanced enough, it has also an artistic and religious character. After the defense functions are disposed of, government becomes largely a regulation of economic programs. Thus the government of modern Denmark is essentially a co-operative dairying association. Kings measured their success in terms of crops. One Egyptian king sang:

> *I was the one who collected the grain*
> *and loved the harvest god.*
> *The Nile greeted me in every valley;*
> *None was hungry in my years,*
> *None thirsted then;*
> *Men dwelt in peace, through which I*
> *wrought, conversing of me.*

Not only did the Nile moisten the land but it bore the wheat to the cities. All day long under the sun's glare, men toiled at the oars of the river barges carrying the tributes of wheat to the Pharaoh. It is supposed by some that the keeping of the tribute tally on the house walls was the origin of writing. Geometry was invented to resurvey the fields after the recession of each flood. As was natural, Egyptian invention and science grew out of the regional problems. Hydraulic engineering made great advances. Great walled-in basins held flood waters so that they could be used for irrigation. Flood gauges were in common use. At Memphis a flood of less than 16 cubits on the gauge (a cubit was about 20 inches) meant insufficiency. Some lands were not flooded, and then some people starved. It must be significant that the first sixteen Arabic numbers are named after the angels of death. That the hymns told of the flood is not surprising. One runs:

"*Hail Hapi* (the Nile), *who doth rise on this earth and comest to give life to Egypt. Who hidest thy coming in darkness on this day when we sing thy coming, a wave spreading over the orchards which Ra* (the sun) *made, to give life to all who thirst, and refusing to water the desert with the overflowings of the waters of heaven. When thou dost descend Geb* (the earth) *is in love with bread, Nefri* (the corn god) *presents his offering. Phtah* (god of labor) *makes every workshop prosper. Do his fingers ail, are they idle?* (Is there no flood?) *Then all the millions of beings are wretched.*

Does he grow less in the sky? (Rain fails.) *Then the gods, themselves, perish, and man; beasts go mad and the earth, great and small, is in torment. But if the prayers of men are granted when he rises* (more than 16 cubits) *then the earth shouts for joy, every belly makes glad, every back is shaken with laughter, every tooth munches."* This is indeed a theme for a symphonic setting, though what instrument would do the munching, I do not know. But *what* a bacchanalian ending.

Attention has been called to the frail, elongate form of the strip of soil which made up the Egyptian political entity. If we consider the delta a lotus blossom then upper Egypt is the stem. It was more a geographic fact than human determination that kept the country together, for the Nile was a perfect artery. The Nile was the main street.

There was, indeed, a feudal period in Egyptian history when local authority was stronger than the central rule, but it was an interlude. The current carried authority. Upstream the agents of the king merely set their sails to catch the quiet, persistent northern wind. This wind, called the Etesian, came from the desert. Deserts are warm and therefore sites of permanent low pressure areas. Winds blow toward low pressures. Hence, the Etesian.

Now Egypt, of course, never lived entirely isolated. She had foreign trade. The island of Crete was probably an Egyptian colony. But since Egypt had no materials for ships they probably used Phoenician or Cretan bottoms. Phoenicia was an industrial country with access to materials foreign to the land of Cheme. Hence Phoenicia sold many things to Egypt, particularly wooden articles. Joseph's brothers appeared before him as Chief Steward to buy grain. We have a quaint pride testified to in the record of one Egyptian who traded with Yam, which was in southern Nubia, a record from 2600 B.C.:

"I descended with 300 asses laden with incense, ebony, grain, panthers (I suppose skins), *ivory, throwstick and every good produce. I was more vigilant than any caravan conductor who had been sent to Yam before."*

It was the Hyksos invasion of 1600 B.C. that opened Egyptian eyes to a greater world. The Hyksos, riding horses, came out of Arabia, conquered Egypt, then lost control—a nomadic interlude. But they taught the Egyptians the use of the horse, the availability of the Suez gateway, and the possibilities of imagination. Shortly, as Egyptian history goes, Palestine and Syria heard the thunder of Egyptian chariots. Any provincialism with high isolation tends towards that aforementioned crystallization of culture, which means a conservatism, and a conventionalizing amounting to stagnation. There was a deal of convention in early Egyptian art and thought and a lack of the vitality present in sixth century Greece.

How shall I illustrate this? The early and central Egyptian religious myth involves a love triangle watched by the father god, the Sun. The story is one of the mystery of love and life. The fertile earth is the woman. Her lover is the Nile flood, and the product of their union is the bounty of the land. The desert wind is the villain. He cuts the hero into sixteen pieces (sic), and then the love of woman rebuilds the hero, and the rhythm of life is repeated. These ideas were not moral, and had, as the Egyptians later put it, no "maat," no righteousness. They were merely savage, amoral wonderings at the mystery of life. Such ideas were highly conventionalized, ritualized, by the priests. It was not until the imperialistic period that new values and pure abstractions came to the Egyptians from Eastern contacts. These culminated in the leadership of Ikhnaton, at once a king and a messiah. For twenty-five years he conquered local provincialism with the idea of a universal or at least a non-agricultural god. But in spite of the foreign contacts and the spirituality of Ikhnaton the strong provincial influences prevailed. The Egyptian hoeman returned to his provincial symbols. He returned to the worship of what was concrete in his milieu, the soil, the sun and the floods. Life for the peasant has always been objective.

Perhaps isolation is the most intriguing of the geographic factors. There is an English-controlled area in the Himalayas, back of Kashmir, which is so difficult of access as to discourage visitors, and where the resources of hospitality as endowed by nature are so slight that there is sufficient surplus to feed only twelve visitors a year. On the other hand, people may live lives apart because of very slight barriers. Off one of the Maine peninsulas, an island lies but a gun shot from the shore, but passage over the narrow water strip is constantly interrupted by tides and storms. The islanders kept so much to themselves that the government was forced to remove part of the population because of inbreeding.

Another such island is the Île aux Coudres in the estuary of the St. Lawrence River. It is barely separated from the mainland, but the passage is marked by a swift tidal rip. The islanders, as I knew them, seldom made the trip, but instead used large boats to go thirty full miles to Quebec, perhaps annually, when potatoes were ready for market. The result was that the culture of the St. Lawrence region, as described at the opening of this volume, was here crystallized and epitomized. The region is an area of cultural retardations, and on this island that retardation is intensified.

Swamp lands have a way of life apart from their surroundings. There is a group of Wends (non-Germans) living in some swamps not far from Berlin. The tiny region is known as the Spreewald. Either race or lowland has been sufficient to preserve here a quaintness which makes the area the delight of Berliners on vacation. The little region has more canals than Venice. The people go to market or a wedding march, or take the cow to the field—in boats. In central Spain is a group of hills of no great magnitude but some confusion, occupied by the Jurdes. The Jurdes were at last report actually savages though surrounded by civilization. Franco may have put them into uniforms, which would represent modernization if not civilization.

The grand example of European isolation lies in the huge marshes of Pinsk. These great expanses of wet lands lie on what was until recently the Russian-Polish border. Miss Semple first called my attention to them when she reported that there were people living there who were so primitive as never to have seen a timepiece. The Polish government recently taking inventory of the marshes, discovered villages previously unknown to the outside world. But exact knowledge comes to us from the pen and camera of Louise A. Boyd.* Pinsk with thirty-two thousand inhabitants has a railroad with one train a day each way, a dirt road usually impassable, and canals. The canals are frozen in winter. All about is a level horizon of monotonous and somber marshes. Silence is broken only by canoe paddles, a rare steamboat whistle or the call of the duck. Among the fisher folk and farmers there is little laughter † or song, and the most characteristic aspect of the marsh

* See "Polish Countrysides," American Geographical Society, Special Publication No. 20 and "The Marshes of Pinsk," *Geographical Review,* Vol. XXVI. (1936) pp. 376-395. These are excellent representations of a culture apart.

† Frequently low monotonous landscape does not seem conducive to laughter. On the low-lying Hallig Islands, off the German coast, laughter is taken as a sign of drunkenness.

dwellers' culture is the grace and skill with which they navigate their boats through the confusing water channels.

These people have made their life from the materials at hand as truly as did the early Egyptians. The houses, the furniture, the clothing (flax and wool) are indigenous. The plow, it is true, is steel, but the harrow is home-made. Foreign foods consist only of coffee, tea and sugar. Miss Boyd goes on delightfully to tell of the primitive life, but what I want to bring out is that here in a region just off the great Moscow-Warsaw highway is as primitive a life as exists anywhere in Europe.

Nor does one need to go to remote lands for isolation. As we have said, barriers are not all physical. Brittany is the northwest corner of France. It is in a physical sense slightly isolated. Brest is the best of French harbors, but it is not a first-rate port. Cherbourg, Le Havre, Nantes and Bordeaux all have greater transfer of tonnage. The reason is its slight remoteness. It is not linear remoteness but a social and economic aloofness. The Bretons are the true Celts of France. Until recently, and to some extent still, the peasant language was Breton, not French. A Breton going to Paris said that he was going to France.

How has this provincialism been maintained? Why were the Bretons not completely melted into the French alloy? One may ascribe this largely to racial standoffishness. True, geologically, Brittany is the New England of France. Its soil is based upon metamorphic and granitic rocks rather than the loosely consolidated rocks of the nearby Paris Basin or the alluviums of the Loire valley. The gray skies offer drizzling rains all winter and much of the summer. Here, in a nation proud of its wheat harvest, the wheat does least well, but there are grass lands and the production of cattle for beef. In one resource alone Brittany stands foremost, for they know the sea. Bretons are more of the sea than the land; most of the French navy is recruited from Brittany. Upon the sardine catch hangs the prosperity of 80,000 Bretons. So this land, smelling of sea industries, with a very moderate prosperity from tillage activities, faces westward. Many of its men know Norway, Iceland and Newfoundland far better than they know the country fifty miles inland.

But all in all, Brittany is not France. For this reason the Parisians flock to its sea-side to live among maritime picturesqueness, Druid ruins, pagan *pardons,* archaic customs and dances as primitive as can be found in Europe, all with signs of a Celtic origin. Here is a strong provincialism whose elements of preservation are due largely to another way of life rather than great remoteness and markedly distinctive physical circumstances.

Let me describe briefly the Île aux Moines as the epitome of Breton life. Curiously shaped like a cross, it lies in the gulf of Morbihan not far from the famous Druid *alignments* at Carnac. It was itself a Druid center. Its peace and seclusion have indeed something religious about it. Here are Breton speech, meals cooked over the hearth (largely sea food), straw-thatched houses with dirt floors, serenity and remoteness from the violent stream of modern affairs. The Île aux Moines is twice a day separated from the mainland by the violent tidal current known as The Wolf. It is to Brittany what Île aux Coudres is to French Canada, but it is not really far removed from the centers of civilization. These sudden changes in ways of life are rapid cultural gradients.

There are few actually remote places left. I have a friend who twice has crossed the Andes and made his way out through the Amazonian jungle. He was the first explorer to enter certain regions, yet there had always been some white man before him, some peddler of firearms or tin pots. While the world was acclaiming Admiral Byrd in Antarctica, geographers were more interested in the work of Bertram Thomas, a scholar, who was traversing the last unknown portion of inhabited land to be explored. This was the Unknown Quarter, the southeast corner of Arabia lying east of the little-known cities of Hadramaut. Of course, many areas are still but slightly known. Though one can hire a seat in a tractor automobile to cross the western Sahara from the Atlas Mountains to Timbuktu (when the desert men are not on raid), in the eastern Sahara there is an actual approximation to "Lost Horizon." This is in the oasis of Kufra in the Libyan Desert, the

headquarters of the religious sect of the Senussi. A
German named Rohlfs, the first westerner to visit the
oasis, arrived in 1879, but the man never returned. In
1921 the charming and fearless Rosita Forbes in com-

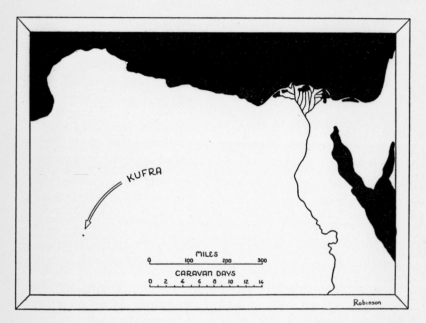

Fig. 12. Kufra is more nearly like Shangri-La than any
other place in the world today. Our lost oasis is indicated
by the smallest dot possible.

pany with A. M. Hassanein, F.R.G.S. and a graduate
of Balliol, reached this lonely "island," but neither
seems to have lost perspective in any way.*

In the leadership of the Senussi is wisdom as mystic

* See "Further Readings" at the end of this volume.

and venerable as any found at Shangri-La. Hassanein's description of the library there fairly makes your mind surge. The room is literally full of books of eastern lore, manuscripts from India, Cairo and Morocco. Hassanein indicates that such mysticism as is found in them should be read only in the vast solitude found there. He would be unhappy to see them read in the western world with its noise and interruptions. There is a lost horizon, there is the living past.

Chapter Seven

ENFORCED RESTLESSNESS

THE USE OF NATURAL RESOURCES DOES NOT ALWAYS lead to sedentary, and hence provincial, forms of culture. A large portion of the land surface of this world of ours is too dry for farming by simple procedures. In modern times tillage has encroached upon semi-arid and even arid land by dry-farming and irrigation, but in earlier days the dry lands offered in support of human life only the wild grass or desert plant as forage for herds. With the domestication of animals as cattle, buffalo, sheep, goats, asses, horses, yaks, and reindeer, men occupied the romantic grasslands, eternally wandering as their beasts sought greener pastures. Literally man choosing to live on the open plains has been "condemned" to mobility, condemned in terms of his primitive state of culture and inventiveness. The word "condemned" does not imply determinism. Let man intelligently advance his inventiveness and he overcomes environmental domination; witness, his practice of dry-farming. But for centuries he merely followed his herds and in many parts of the world does so today.

These grasslands, steppes and deserts are exceedingly widespread and spacious. Flanking tropical jungles are savannas, with rain only in summer, which run from tillage land at jungle margins to pure desert in higher latitudes. The Sudan is an example as are the veldt, llanos, campos, or dry moors. In higher latitudes in continental interiors far from marine influences there are steppes. Our high plains are an example. North of the tree line the plains in summer are covered with flowering grasses and in winter support green moss and lichen. These are the tundra, the reindeer country. Except where locally there are oases, these various areas have not produced provincial ways of living. Instead, herding country has enforced a restlessness upon men, has created nomadism.

All of us were taught in our early geography about the nice homes on the canal barges of Holland, how the little cabin was so neat, the brass so well polished and the geranium at the window so red. Today many of the barges are less domestic and more dirty because women no longer live aboard: the Dutch government decreed that children and their mothers could live on the barges only in the summer. In the winter they were to remain fixed in one place so the children could go to school. Fixity makes for accumulation and organization of experience. Wandering means a scattering of experience. Nomads are wanderers. The most pungent remark made of nomads is that "though they are always on the move, they never progress."

Yet the term wanderer is not quite exact in describing the nomad. There is nothing vague about his journeys. Since he must live he is impelled in this direction or that to find grass for his herds with as much force as the seasons demonstrate in the lives of the tillers. Take the Kirghiz, the most renowned nomads of modern times.* The Kirghiz at the opening of the twentieth century occupied loosely and temporarily areas which extend from the mountains about Lake Balkash to the low grass plains of the lower Volga. In summer the mountain pastures called them almost as by magnetism. The tribes and their herds were in summer to be found in the high, cool plateaus and mountain shelves where green forage was plentiful. With the approach of winter, the first storm that shook their *yurts* (huts of hide on a flimsy framework of wands) was a signal for the move, the annual trek to the steppes of Transcaspia. The beasts were rounded up, the baggage, dismantled

* Modernization of Siberia by the Soviets has profoundly changed the nomadic ways of the Kirghiz.

yurts, pots and boxes were fastened to the sides of the camels or cattle; horses were for riding alone. The slower sheep and goats were sent first down the rocky trails. Then, following the dust of the sheep herds, the full procession began: camels accompanied by the women and children, herds of cattle bellowing protest, riders on horses shouting; a great surge of life, men and their beasts driven as much by instinct as intelligence, driven almost as a flight of locusts. The flight was hundreds of miles in length and ranged from the Pamir meadows fifteen thousand feet above the level of the sea, to the salt desert of the Caspian actually below sea level.

Such restlessness is one of the great historical motives. Scythians, Avars, Huns, Saracens, Tartars, Mongols, Turks, Kurds; it has always been the same. They were the have-nots of history. Let their grasslands dry, or a pest come among the cattle, and men fought their way into those fat lands where food was available. Living precariously upon the milk of their herds, endowed with mobility, and taught cruelty by the natural severity of their life, they were almost invincible. The chief of defenses which the lowly tillers could offer were fortified cities (the walls of Babylon are said to have been 300 feet high), or huge stone barriers that ran across the countryside. The greatest was the Chinese wall built against the Mongols. Persia built the Red Wall one hundred and fifty miles in length as a barrier against the Huns. The Crimean Peninsula was completely guarded against the Scythians by a similar defense. In a more modern period border nomads were organized by sedentaries as a defense against other nomads. The best known examples are the alliances between the tsars of Russia and the Don Cossacks.

The historical role of these hordes so loosely attached to the land has been one of destruction. There was Attila, the Scourge, and Tamarlane, the Earth Shaker. How much their destructive inroad on civilization was due to impelling forces of hunger, and how much was due to the attraction of easy living in the sedentary centers, cannot now be told. Nomads do not write records. We do not even know today the location of the vast tent city of Karakorum, somewhere on the southern slopes of the Tian Shan. The waving grass of the steppes soon obliterates the passage of the nomad, as the winds spread sand over hoof marks. But the nomad had another role which did aid civilization. It was he, as a soldier or caravan leader, who carried habits, inventions and ideas across the waste spaces. To illustrate this: the Babylonians were followers of the plow, they rode to war in chariots, they studied the stars, they held in veneration images of the winged bull, and they were familiar with crocodiles in their rivers. Babylonians came in contact with nomadic Scythians from Russia and Asia, who had the pleasant habit of drinking out of the skulls of their enemies.

The first civilization of northern China appeared in one of those protected "cradles" so favorable for civilization, the valley of the Wei Ho, a tributary of the Hwang. Invaders out of the west settled in this valley. These strangers used the plow, they rode to war in chariots, they studied astronomy, they worshiped the winged bull, they had veneration for dragons—and they had the pleasant habit of drinking out of the skulls of their enemies.

Few have written comprehensively upon pastoral nomads of the steppes and deserts since Ibn Khaldun (about 1400), and his writings had an unfortunate propensity for being destroyed by fire and salt water. One of our best authorities is Marco Polo, and there is the Bible. The story of the Near East is a series of histories, separate histories of separate geographical entities. First, it is the story of Babylonia, the story of successive waves of nomads who settled in the great oasis and were attracted to agricultural and then urban life by the natural resources of soil and flood. Then there was Assyria, a land of have-nots. As leaders arose to organize the half-starved Assyrians they descended upon the lands where date and grain and ground-fruit made men fat, came down in fierce hordes from a land that taught no mercy. And lastly there is the immortal story of a little people who wandered along the green fringes almost literally begging. They were uninspired until the appearance of Moses, but finally they forced themselves upon the land of Canaan and mixed with the people of the plains. What happened to these nomadic tribes as they became agriculturists we shall see.

The Near East is a story of the surge and resurge of
enforced restlessness. The Israelites themselves were in
their habits of life no different from the other Semitic
desert tribes. Their morality alone distinguished them;
without a Moses we might never have heard of them.
But their important history, aside from their moral
teachings, is the story of a transition from wandering
to the sedentary life of the tiller. Economically and
psychologically there was a profound change.

This history of the Near East is not simple to follow.
Except for a few properly-minded students, the names
Babylonia, Elam, the Hittites, Nebuchadnezzar, Sen-
nacherib, Nineveh, the Medes (and the Persians), Solomon and Sheba mean one thing or another, but they
mean very little in relation to each other. Only assyri-
ologists and other thick-glassed gentlemen can be expected to know the sequence of kings who ruled the
ancient East. My first personal clarification of the Bible
story came from reading Lewis Brown's "The Graphic
Bible," which has a map for every page. So let me draw
a map of the ancient East and a map of the grass or
fields in those countries, and I shall hope thus to
straighten you out on your ancient history. These maps
are to be based largely upon the distribution of green
grass. The oldest motif, the oldest human cry of groups,
is "greener grass." Do you remember how Lot and
Abraham, not able to find green grass sufficient for
their camels, separated? Lot chose to become a city
dweller and Abraham stuck to the nomad ideals. The

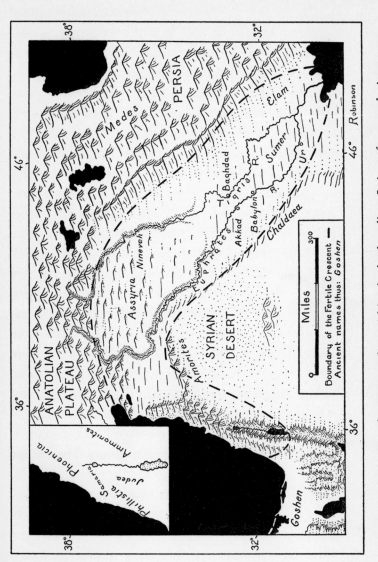

Fig. 13. The Fertile Crescent lies within the broken line. It is unfortunately impossible to put seven millenniums of events on a 3½ by 5 map.

severity of herding on meager pastures brought forth
the strict discipline and high moral values of the
Hebrews. Were not the prophets during the soft, fat
days of agriculture continually calling upon their people
to return to the herding ideology?

On map, page 127, if you pass out of Egypt through
Goshen and skirt the northern edge of the desert, Philistia and Palestine, and then Phoenicia lie along the
route you travel. Then, by the Syrian Saddle, go through
Syria (Naharin). Turning south again, traverse Assyria
and Babylonia. Most coasts, especially those backed by
highlands, have rain even though they lie in desert regions. Philistia, the highlands of Judea and Samaria, as
well as Palestine, had some rain. On our map let us color
them light green. Phoenicia and the high, rain-collect-
ing Lebanons should also be a light green. To the
north of our route is the quite elevated Anatolian
plateau. In this Mediterranean area there are rain-
giving storms in winter due to the southern shift of
the westerly winds in that season. These highlands are
elevated enough to have snow. In summer time the
melting snow feeds streams which, descending to the
plain, lose themselves in the desert sands and in doing
so keep green a piedmont strip.

We have come to the north-south land of Mesopotamia, the land between the rivers. The northern half
is an upland; the southern a delta plain. The two
rivers are the Euphrates and the Tigris. They influenced the upland not at all for they were incised in

gorges. This upland is a steppe land, light green due to winter rains. In ancient days a few meager farming areas were scattered about. One, Assir, gave the name Assyria to the whole upland. The delta plain was Babylonia, annually flooded by the melting snows of Anatolia. Irrigation canals extended the service of the water. This land of verdure and prolific returns from the soil, like Egypt, should be a dark green on our map. But, unlike Egypt, there should not be a definite line between the green and the desert brown. The colors should be blended into each other, a gradual transition. The green areas, light or dark, extending from the Red Sea to the Persian Gulf are known in history as the Fertile Crescent.

Babylonia had a history contemporaneous with Egypt. Moreover, it was similar because of its development of agriculture. It was even more dependent upon the date palm, which not only provided food for man and beast, but gave shade against evaporation and so protected smaller plants, grain, vegetables and tree fruits. Herodotus, traveling through miles of palm groves, gave an almost unbelievable account of the fertility. The land supported a dense population and yet had an enormous agricultural surplus. There were, however, definite wants.

Babylonia had no wood, no stone, and no mineral resources, and the people were sheltered by mud houses. There seems to be some soul-expressing need of peoples as they become great to build tangible evidence of their greatness. I am thinking of the temples, palaces and, if you will, the hanging gardens. And people of the plains have an urge to build towers to lift themselves above the earthly monotony. This was seen in Babylon and is seen in Columbus, Ohio, or Tulsa, Oklahoma. So the Babylonians accomplished their monuments by means of flat, slab-like bricks. Clay was used in a multitude of fashions from the clay sickles to the cylindrical writing tablets; even their art was merely sculpture in bas-relief on terra cotta. Yet in that problem lay the simple basis of a foreign commerce; food stuffs could be traded for wood, stone and metals. Traffic was active on the two rivers and along the valleys. Ships left Persian Gulf ports, best known to us through Sinbad the Sailor, and sailed for India.

One great pulse through Babylonian history was the continuous raid and invasion by the nomad. Desert nomads are always near starvation. The Arabian desert, unlike the Libyan, was inhabited. Surge after surge of peoples, peaceful and warlike, were attracted by the "fat land" of the river plains. The first great invaders were the Sumerians who settled in the swamp of the southern delta and introduced agriculture. Their capital was Sumer. Another invading group was the Akkadians who founded Akkad. They conquered the Sumerians but were conquered by the strong Sumerian culture.

Another wave came out of Syria, the Amorites. They founded Babylon on the curve of the Euphrates where it is nearest to the Tigris. So important is that situation that though the *exact* site has never been the same there has always been a city of importance in the same general neighborhood. The present city is Bagdad. These recurring invasions of Babylonia make up most of the political events in its history, which is a geographic story.

Assyria was quite another matter, a barren land given over largely to nomads. Nomads have mobility and endurance valuable in warfare. They have little property and less fixity, which gives them a military advantage over the sedentaries who must each stand to defend a farmyard. Moreover, harsh conditions teach nomads cruel necessity which advances them in war. "And the Assyrians came down like wolves on the fold." There was Babylon destroyed by the Assyrians. The Babylonians rose again to power only when they enlisted other nomads, the Medes, to help them attack and destroy the stone walls of Nineveh, the Assyrian capital on the Tigris.

The basic theme of the ancient history of the Near East is a struggle for grass. Each king measured his influence, each country measured its wealth, in terms of how much of the Fertile Crescent it held. Little Palestine with its sub-marginal existence in a land which we must color a pale green on our map, never was of political consequence nor did it have wealth, except during the reign of Solomon when a small portion of the Crescent was organized and consolidated.

Men have fought through the centuries for bread and booty: the "bread" of the nomad was largely the wild date and *koumiss*. *Koumiss* is the soured curds of herd milk, and milk is but converted grass.

Not that it proves anything about the Near East, but I used to talk to the drifters in our Southwest, sad-eyed wanderers who often spend a year desultorily working a farm only to move on after each harvest. Nomads. I met them walking beside their crazy little covered wagons drawn by weak horses, and I asked them why they moved, where they were going. The usual answer was, "Wal, stranger, going South this year. Lookin' for greener grass."

The Israelites knew the Fertile Crescent throughout its length. Their earliest history is a story of just such a search for pasture. The original Israelites were desert-folk, nomads who tended their flocks, and eked out a barren existence in the dry lands. Their home was somewhere in the desert from which all Semites sprang. Like themselves, their tribal god, Jehovah, was a wanderer, ever searching for green pastures for his people, revealing himself in a storm-cloud, or out of a burning bush, or on a desert mountain-top. Perhaps, under the leadership of their legendary patriarch, Abraham, the Israelites tried to find a home for themselves in the city of Ur, but, dissatisfied, moved out into the desert again. Sometime before 1500 B.C. their wanderings brought them to the heights that looked down upon the

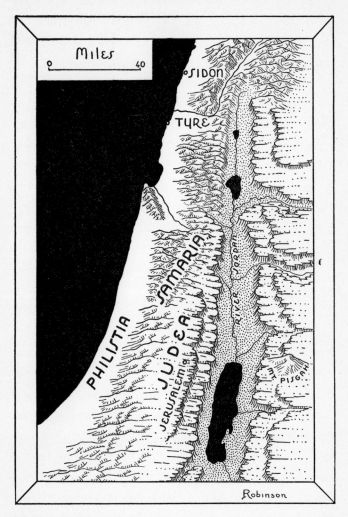

Fig. 14. Topography of Bible Lands. Remember that the
Dead Sea is 1300 feet below the level of the Mediterranean.

green plains of Palestine, the land of Canaan. But these plains were then secure under Egyptian rule, and there was no place for the Israelites. Facing starvation without grass for the herds, they sought refuge in Egypt. At least they found food, but a king of Egypt treated them harshly. Under the leadership of Moses, they left Egypt, and wandered for years in the peninsula of Sinai and in the land southeast of the Jordan. Finally Moses took his people to the top of Mount Pisgah, in the land of Moab east of Palestine, and showed them the land of Canaan in the Jordan Valley. The Israelites had at last found green pastures. It was the Promised Land.

This Promised Land was a part of the Fertile Crescent, with the valley of the Jordan a green depression lying between two highlands that paralleled the coast. (Map No. 14.) The river rose in the north, flowed through the Sea of Galilee, across dry plains, and thence down into the Dead Sea. Toward the northern end of Palestine, the western highland had a break through which the agricultural plains of the Jordan stretched seaward. At the western extremity of the break, overlooking the Mediterranean, stood Mount Carmel, marking the dividing point between the coast-country of Phoenicia to the north and the coast-country of Philistia to the south. The highlands east of Phoenicia were the Lebanon Mountains, famous for cedar trees. The highlands east of Philistia were called Samaria and Judea; Samaria, a rough country of hills, the land of the vine and the olive; Judea, a plateau with an occasional valley, good only for sheep.

(Nomads ordinarily contribute little to cultural history.) But there was some unaccountable genius in these wandering Hebrews which cannot be explained but must be acknowledged. In the Bible we can see stages of development and advancement in spirituality. In the beginning Jehovah, the god of the Israelites, was not god of the world but merely the deity of a wandering tribe. This god, like that of the desert Assyrians, was one to be feared. He was cruel, jealous and merciless. In his name, the Israelites butchered whom they could. He was "Jehovah of the Armies," and he smote enemies, even to children. Only the Israelites did he love.

Later, when the Israelites settled in the Promised Land, ease softened their religious ideas. Many times did the faithful lose a certain moral discipline that had been theirs on the march. We have a saying today that Bedouins (Arabs) rot in the towns, and the prophets Amos and Micah were constantly exhorting the Israelites to go back to the morals of desert life. Gradually community life had its effects. Men must live together in peace. The world was not cruel but kindly. It is first in the teachings of Hosea that God is looked upon as the friend of man. It only remained for Jesus to provide the concept of God as a spirit prizing brotherly love above all virtues.

Not only did physical circumstance enter into the concept of the god-head, but it trailed through all the religious symbolism. Ever-present in Palestinian life were sheep, and the shepherds watched their sheep with tenderness. Isaiah says:

He will feed his flock like a shepherd,
He will gather the lambs in his arm,
And carry them in his bosom,
And will gently lead those that have their young.

This tending of sheep was of the utmost importance in the life of the Judean. On the highlands men spent lonely night watches with their herds under such brilliant stars as few readers of this book have seen. Their vigils gave them time to think; their religious traditions gave them food for thought.

The meager pasture lands kept before them constantly the need for greener grass. The psalms show again and again the influence of herding and the starry night-watches with the sheep. "The Lord is my shepherd, I shall not want." A master in their eyes was a shepherd, and always in a land of such meager food supply, want was a cloud that hung over them. "He maketh me to lie down in green pastures" ... the search for greener grass. "He leadeth me beside the still waters" ... the desert pool. "He restoreth my soul." The tired shepherd welcomed the chance for rest in a place where there was grass and water. Here for a while his flock would browse and he be free to meditate on God and nature. "He leadeth me in the paths of righteousness." Was not the desert man in fear of being lost? "Thou preparest a table before me in the presence of mine enemies." Every fugitive knew that by unwritten law he could find food and shelter in a shepherd's tent. Anointing with oil was pleasant because it kept the skin soft in so dry a climate. "And I shall dwell in the house of the Lord forever." Do you remember the line "I would rather be a door-keeper in the house of the Lord than live in the tents of the ungodly"? One does not have to go far to find evidence that the whole of the Israelite symbols of religion grew out of the world as they knew it.

The Israelites illustrate better than any other people how the transition from nomadism to agriculture was made. We find them owning land, and learning the wealth that lay in land, seizing more land. The Golden Age of Israel was the age of the greatest commerce. Parallel with the change in the economic life came a change in moral philosophy. It is a simple and direct story.

The story of the Fertile Crescent is one of nomads who ferociously claimed the lands blessed with rain or flood, even though the water supplied was pitifully scanty. It is the story of how these herders became tillers and stood to defend their fields. It is the story of lands of few resources and of the caravan commerce that equalized the inequality of resources. "Restlessness" is, for the people of desert or steppe, "Kismet."

Chapter Eight

THE SEA AS A

PROVINCE

Land travel is a weary affair. Kipling describes the terrible fatigue, the monotony of tired step after step, in "Boots." Even when beasts carried the burden, men walked. What a liberation the ship was! Great bulk and great weight could be moved by oar or sail. The invention of the ship was an early matter, so ancient that in widely scattered parts of the earth the root-word for boat is the same. It is "Nao." We have it in "navy." A raft is a simple device to get out to better fishing grounds or cross a river. Put a blade on your pole or flatten your spear head and you have an oar.

Put sides on the raft and you have a barge. Stand up and spread out your cape and you have a sail. The keel was, however, an intellectual invention.

In early times on the Mediterranean there were two kinds of boats, the round boat and the long boat. The round boat was a barge, with a curved but scarcely pointed front, which moved by a sail or with oar-sweeps as auxiliary power. The long boat was propelled by oars with a sail as auxiliary. Galleys were in use down to the seventeenth century. They were adapted to the Mediterranean which for weeks may be almost without wind. I have spent lazy days on the shores of that sea watching the round boats, hardly changed in design for two thousand years, lying idle on the water waiting for some little breeze to move them gently towards their goal. The round boat was a freight carrier. The galley was for passengers, mainly fighters. Navies consisted of long boats because they could maneuver better.

Early sailing was coastwise. The boats went barely beyond the reefs that marked the approach to the shore. The coast-line of all but the lesser bays was followed minutely. Some few routes struck across the open sea. One of the best accounts of this type of sailing happens to be by a Japanese, the "Diary of Tosca Nikki," a delightful experience for any reader. It tells how a governor returned to the capital. The two hundred miles were covered by boat in fifty-five days, though every night the ship was hauled ashore, and on many days the sailors did not put out because of high waves or high living the night before.

Who shall say who were the first sailors on the Mediterranean? Among the first were the Phoenicians, Semites who took to the sea. Phoenicia lay on a mildly fertile plain between the Lebanon Mountains and the sea. Back of the mountains lay a sterile hinterland. On the land, therefore, there was no opportunity for expansion. The Phoenicians lived, as it were, in a theater with the sea for a stage, and the cedars of Lebanon furnished material for ships. As the plain became overpopulated, the most natural expansion was by sea.

And the Cretans began sailing as early as 3000 B.C. and continued until the middle of the second millennium. Crete is a large island south of Greece which closes in the Aegean Sea on the south. It was inhabited in the "gray dawn of history," perhaps first by Philistines or Egyptians, but in any case the earliest major settlement was at Phaestum on the south shore facing Egypt. Later when the island's commercial interests turned to the Aegean, Cnossus on the north shore became the chief center. These were the first cities of Europe.

I have a theory, more sentimental than scientific, which is that the sea creates a joyous spirit. This is not proven and exists merely as an idea. Nevertheless, islands do afford protection from enemies. So these were the first people who joyously lifted their eyes from the ground, the first people to be free of taboos. They had no slavery of the mind, and knew the vast sense of freedom that comes with standing before the sail on the prow of a ship. The wide, clean sea flooded all their imagination.

But I really become enthusiastic about human nature when I consider the Achaeans. Those Danubians migrated to the Aegean shores and became the first Greeks, and they were the heroes of the Homeric legends. My theory of maritime-born happiness finds good support in them. Living semi-nomadic lives in forest glades, they were irrepressibly drawn to the sea, and born of their sea adventure came a new lust for life. They laughed as the fresh wind bore them toward new shores and new adventures, and their gods laughed with them. Imagine Jehovah or Moloch laughing!

The Phoenicians once controlled the traffic of the Aegean Sea. Then the Cretans and the ill-fated people of Troy fought to control that market for their rude manufactures. We do not know who destroyed Cretan Cnossus, but it is legendary that the Achaeans, after a ten-year siege, destroyed the city of Troy.*

Helen, I have no doubt, was quite beautiful. But there were not nearly a thousand ships, the towers of Ilium were scarcely topless, and we are not certain of Helen. Indeed, for many a century it had been the practice of the Phoenicians to purloin Greek women. Helen was

* For this interpretation of legends see the readable "Homer and History" and "Troy, A Study of Homeric Geography" by Walter Leaf.

no more the cause of the Trojan War than the killing of the Archduke at Sarajevo was the cause of the first World War.

There were nine cities of Troy, archaeologically piled in burnt ruins upon each other. Helen lived in number six. Each of the nine cities for some reason was attacked. A plausible but not necessarily correct explanation involves commercial geography. The Greeks were seamen, as Plato said, like frogs about a pond, always ready to jump in. They thought of the Aegean as their own, and they sailed beyond into the Black Sea to get gold and fish and to buy wheat from a land that still is a granary. Now the passage from the Aegean to the Black Sea is always by the Dardanelles, a swift east-to-west current. Navigators in those days waited for a favorable wind, especially against currents. (Remember how Virgil repeats, "Favorable winds having been obtained, they set sail.") So the Greek ships would lie at anchor or on a sandy strip just south of the mouth of the Dardanelles for days or even weeks waiting for a following wind. Just a league back from this anchorage was a city of non-Greeks, who delighted in raiding the Greek ships. These rascals were the Trojans, the only enemy of complete Greek control of the Aegean. Naturally, Troy was repeatedly destroyed. Helen was just an excuse, for the real cause of the wars against Troy was for the control of sea commerce.

After the Achaeans, there came other waves of migrants from the Danube Valley. Two peoples, the

Ionians and Dorians, were particularly distinctive. Strange that the Danube Valley should have bred the wonderful Greeks. Or were they so distinctive before they settled on Aegean shores? Was there something inherent in their new milieu to develop their quality of mind? It is much safer to say that the marvelous quality of Greek culture was the result of racial mutations rather than that it was induced by contact with the sea. On the other hand, nothing would please the geographer more than to discover that the clear air in which the mountains stood out with such startling definity combined with the cosmopolitan contacts of the sea to bear the thoughtful Socrates, or the creative Phidias. There is little that can be said about geographic factors in Greek character, but that little let me say, not so much as a demonstration of geographic factors but as a definition of the limits of those factors.

The Aegean Sea was a school for sailors, for the mountains waded into the sea to their knees. There was no continuous coastal plain, and the ancients did not willingly climb mountains. They thought of peaks as the homes of the gods. Communication between the little intermontaine plains was often easiest by sea. Between the digital mountains were coves and bays, not frightening to the naval experimenter as an open sea would have been. And islands, easily within sight, tempted the early sailor out to sea as stepping stones. And the sea itself! No dense fogs, only the haze of a lazy, sun-lit water. No fearful tides or currents, and, except for a few winter months, no storms, unless the gods were angered. One could sail the entire Aegean and seldom be out of sight of headland but for an area of the north. Even there the snow peak of Mount Athos could be seen hanging in the sky above the sea haze. So can we fully understand: "The oar was more important in Greek history than the shepherd's crook." How much the freshness of the sea air actually did to Greek history one can only guess, but if we compare Greece with the countries where men sweat on the hot plains, imaginative stimuli limited by each barley patch, we have a comparative measure.

Another phase of sea influence should be noted. The Aegean is land-bound, a neat sea, well-defined, with certain gateways, a province. A peninsula is certainly a geographic province, so is a sea. Easily crossed, the Aegean was not a barrier between the Balkans and Asia Minor, but rather a connection. The Greeks until a late date did not know the west side of the Balkan peninsula at all, and even today much of the chaotic mountain interior remains backward. Yet the Ionians early migrated to the eastern shore of the sea. Ionia and the very Greek city of Miletus were not in Europe but in Asia Minor. There was no true land of Greece; rather were there littoral settlements around the Aegean.

Ordinarily a good space in Greek histories is given over to the Persian conflict. This is again the matter of the sea; thalassic geography. Persia expanded the greatest land empire of all ancient times. Persians, moreover, were an enlightened people with the first great tolerance in history. Highlanders by origin, they not only conquered the Fertile Crescent but spread over the Anatolian plateau. It was natural that they should fight towards the sea coast to complete their conquest. This meant control of Asiatic Ionia. Ionia was Greek, and Aegean. Either the Greeks should restrain the Persians from control of a portion of the Aegean littoral, or the Persians, once on the shores of the Aegean, would complete their conquest by attacking and conquering the European shores. If one enters a province with an army, conquest of the entire province is definite logic. Hence the march of Xerxes against Athens. On the sea the Persians were out of their element. The Greeks won, as we know, with a wooden wall of ships at Salamis. The Greeks then went on to free the Ionian cities. Only after complete control of the sea was their task completed. This same struggle for the Aegean was repeated after the first World War when the Greeks and Turks fought for Smyrna.

Briefly, in the first chapter, the Adriatic was cited as a province. Rome, Venice and modern Italy have struggled for its control. It was the same consciousness of unity of sea which led the Japanese across their western waters to Chosen and Manchukuo. As this manuscript is being written, the Baltic, North and Black seas are objects of strife, and many nations watch the Mediterranean jealously.

The Baltic, unlike the Mediterranean, has a long axis
that lies across lines of latitude; the climate of one end
is quite different from the other. Moreover, the river-
fed arms, the Gulf of Bothnia and the Gulf of Finland,
are brackish, so these extremities freeze. Russia had
until previously but one port on the Baltic and that is
blocked by ice half the year. This is Kronstadt, the port
of Leningrad. As soon as German co-operation and
acquiescence were obtained, ports in the Baltic countries
were seized upon and islands were taken for defense.
The invasion of Finland apparently had the same
purpose.

The Baltic Sea at one time was under control of the
German Hanseatic League. During the Thirty Years
War it became a Swedish lake. In more modern times
the Germans have controlled the sea commercially, and
their merchants were found in every port. Suddenly,
while German interests were otherwise diverted, Russia
took over control of half of the southern Baltic shore
so surely that Hitler recalled his merchant population
from that littoral, which is an astonishing retreat.

Once King Canute controlled the shores of the North
Sea. At another period the English demanded flag
salute of all boats sailing those waters. So strong was
this maritime control that the English, with no other
justification, shelled the forts about Copenhagen. Germany was then no maritime power at all, but German
industrial growth soon demanded a place on the sea.
German and English struggle for complete and final

control of the North Sea is going forward desperately as this is written.

All of which naturally leads into the absorbing question of sea power. There are many books on this question by naval and commercial experts who are not geographers, but what they write is geography of the first order.

Chapter Nine

GEOGRAPHY BECOMES

MORE COMPLICATED

Regional studies in this volume began with a
chapter on isolation. Ancient Egypt was the chief example selected by way of illustration. Lest the reader
get an idea that all people subjected themselves to continuous influences that were purely local, a chapter followed which spoke, too briefly, of nomadism. This was
the story of the Fertile Crescent. Then the sea as a
province was presented. No better illustration than
ancient Greece is to be found. But life is not so simple;
commerce carries both commodities and ideas. The
chapter on isolation, after all, gave a false picture.

People are beset by foreign ideas, and civilization advances at a rate proportional to outside stimuli. Philosophers and scholars welcome exotic contacts. Locally minded people (we call them nationalists) resist foreign "isms." This is a chapter about extensions of contacts, about the cultural significance of imperialism, and about the social repercussions of widespread commerce. In order to maintain an historical sequence we shall take Rome as the chief illustration, and for a more modern interpretation, we shall turn to the beginnings of the British Empire.

Babylon or Athens or any of the "world" cities of earlier times were, it is true, extra-provincial in culture. Hellenistic Alexandria had a civilization in no way local. It remained, however, for the city of Rome to become truly cosmopolitan. How this cosmopolitanism came about is a story worth telling for the geography that lies in it. Empires that endure for centuries (excluding such interludes as the Napoleonic conquests, of course), have causes which are national. There are fundamental bases of great imperialisms. How was it that Rome came to rule the Mediterranean World and beyond? Certainly it was not merely race ego and the ambition of traders. The Roman Empire was more than a military conquest. It had geographic and commercial functions. All great powers before Rome had been essentially land or sea powers. Rome was both. Rome controlled African desert and northern forest. Rome was extra-geographical in that it bound together so many distinctly different provinces. Yet there was a certain logic in the succession of steps which led from the expansion of the little city on the plains of Latium to its domination of sixty-five million people. This explains the need for parading before you some geographical facts of Roman history, though parades are, as they always have been, a characteristic of Roman life.

There was a group of rustics, dealers in cattle, who lived upon the plain of Latium in central Italy. By the year 1000 B.C. we find these herders and farmers trading with Etruscans who lived across the Tiber River to the north. The Etruscans were a forward people, farmers, iron-workers and sailors. They traded with Greece back in the days of Cretan supremacy. They had a written language, a sense of art, commercial practices, and reputation for mercilessness. So the Latins selected seven hills near the Tiber as a marketplace for trading with the Etruscans. This was Rome and the square market plaza became the Forum.

In 750 B.C. an Etruscan king muscled his way into control of Rome. Two hundred and fifty years later the Romans overthrew the Etruscans and started their own growth. Remember, there is no geographic explanation for Rome's greatness. It was a function of some innate genius of the Roman people or, perhaps, of the Roman leaders. But what were the elements of location and physical circumstance upon which they seized?

Firstly, Rome lay between two interesting civiliza-

Fig. 15. Rome lay between Etruria and the Greek colonies to the south. Thus culturally the city was twice stimulated.

tions; the organized Etruscans on the north, and the less organized but more brilliant Greek colonies at the bottom of the boot of Italy. Twice-stimulated was Rome. The Etruscans taught the first principles of building, the making of aqueducts and road construction. The Greeks taught principles of government, and gave early lessons in art. The two-consul system of the Romans would seem to have been copied from the dual king system of some Greek cities, for the republican form of government was essentially Greek. Location and the implication of location are always a proper subject for a geography.

The first wars of Rome were for self-preservation and, unconsciously, to fulfill the principle that a peninsula tends to come under one power. Latium was not a well-defined province. Italy was. The hill people made raids (for cattle) upon the plains, and the first great struggles, the bloody Samnite Wars, were punitive expeditions against those hill people. As Rome grew, it was natural that there should be a conflict with Etruria. The Greek cities combined against Rome and met defeat. Soon all Italy, except the well-defined Po valley, was a Roman empire. The leaders of Italy might have seen fit to limit Roman expansion to a conquest of the peninsula, for there is nothing in early Roman history that foretold of her great imperialism.

Then Carthage, the Phoenician city of North Africa, entered the picture, and the story becomes essentially commercial. Richest among Carthaginian colonies was

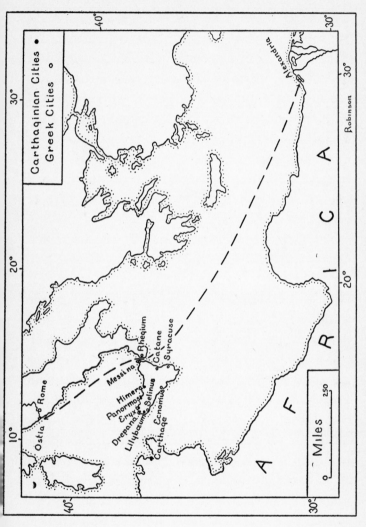

Fig. 16. The Straits of Messina were the critical point on the "life line" of Roman food commerce.

western Sicily, which was extra-Italian. The Romans were not troubled by these Punic possessions, but already Italian productivity was declining. The climate was changing. The soil was becoming exhausted. Food was brought by sea from as far as the perennial Egypt. Rome commercially had outgrown its Italian provincialism. From the Straits of Messina between Italy and Sicily to the harbor of Ostia at the mouth of the Tiber, the sea was white with the sails of grain ships. Therefore, the Romans had given the Carthaginians to understand that they would countenance no settlement upon the shores of the straits. Eastern Sicily was given over to quite independent Greek cities, and these began to quarrel among themselves. Carthage seized this opportunity to expand its control towards and about the straits, so the Romans declared war.

The victory of the first Punic War was Roman: Sicily came under Roman control and Carthage was driven from the sea. Rome had broken from her peninsular provincialism, and, to an extent, became concerned with commerce. Commerce is an aid to imperialistic cohesion.

A vengeful Carthaginian general returning home took his small son before the terrible statue-god Moloch and bade him swear hatred of the Romans. The man was Hamilcar Barca, the stripling was Hannibal. Carthage, losing Sicily, turned its attention to Spain, the Eldorado of the Phoenicians, the Tarshish of the Bible. Hannibal, reaching maturity, was a general on

Spanish soil. As Carthage was beaten on the sea, he determined to march over land to Rome. With thousands of men, and some elephants, he forced his way across two mountain ranges, widening the passes for the elephants, undismayed by stones rolled down on his army by prankish Gauls. He reached Italy and was triumphant. For more than a decade he marched about the Italian peninsula without serious opposition, but one thing seemed too great for him, the storming of the walls of Rome.

Scipio, a new Roman general, arose against Carthage. He had won military honors in Spain, as had Hannibal. He had fought there to cut off the Carthaginian supplies. Now he was sent to Carthage itself and Hannibal went home to defend his native city. After the great battle of Zama, the defeated Hannibal fled to the Near East where he lived and died as a minor trouble maker, a Samson shorn of his locks. Thus ended the Second Punic War. The territorial result was that Carthage lost the Spanish colonies, and Spain became the first truly overseas Roman province, for long the most important commercial province in the empire.

The Third Punic War had no geography or humanity. By trickery Rome justified complete destruction of Carthage and the Carthaginians, a destruction of fear and sadistic cruelty. The three wars together made a land-bound people into a great sea power. The Romans now felt themselves invincible. They had impetus and an unemployed army. As the Greeks had assisted Hannibal, Greece and then the ancient Levant were proper fields for Roman exploitation. The conquest of Cleopatra and the rest of Egypt followed. Personal ambition was back of the conquest of Gaul. In Gaul and Germany and Britain the Roman was out of his element; he knew little of forest environments. For strength of empire the Roman world should have been confined to the Mediterranean basin. But Roman ambition, backed by a genius for organization and military operations, challenged any barrier.

This brings one to a chief means of centralizing authority, the means by which empires are held together, the Roman roads. I can say little about them because of the inadequacy of my descriptions compared to the writings of the authority, Hilaire Belloc. With one of the most delightful styles in English literature, he made a roadway a living past.* A road is a geographic fact, an expression of human needs, of contrasted resources and the conquest of locale. The Roman roads were for foot travel. As such they went straight or nearly straight, as the diagram shows. (Figure 17.) Obliquely over hills, bridging streams, they went directly toward their goal. Marked with mile stones, they gave accurate distances to interior points. The Greek geographers knew only coastlines. The Romans, exactly and usually without philosophic conclusions, improved the cartography of the interior. But

---

* Read Hilaire Belloc's "The Road." J. W. Gregory has an excellent book, "The Story of the Road."

the Roman roads designed for military pedestrians and mounted messengers also served commerce. They helped bind the many provinces into a whole and thus furthered Romanization. The spread of culture is always evidence of a true imperialism.

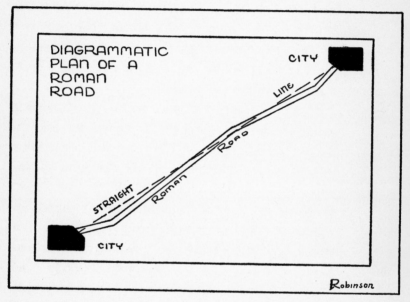

Fig. 17. The Roman roads followed a straight line almost but not exactly. This is after Hilaire Belloc who knows more about roads than any other man.

Commerce tends to become an integrated whole within a political entity. Traders in early days seldom traveled beyond political jurisdictions. Under Caesar Augustus began the Roman peace of two hundred years. Piracy and brigandage were suppressed. Tax collections were more just, coinage more common. Roads were safe, harbors and lighthouses were constructed. Not only did merchants travel from Syria to Lusitania (Portugal), or Numidia (Northern Africa), or Britain in safety but casual Romans made a grand tour of the Mediterranean as a matter of education. Never before had equable laws and freedom from confiscation of goods made commerce with far distant countries so safe and profitable.

Ships sailing out of Alexandria carried many thousands of bushels of grain. Caravans over the hot roads in Spain included hundreds of mules. So great were distances and so complicated was trade that a Roman merchant no longer bought rugs, say, directly from Mesopotamia but purchased them through a broker in Antioch. Antioch, Alexandria, Smyrna, Corinth, Marseille, New Carthage (Spain), and Gades (Cadiz) became collection points, with warehouses and commissionaires. Foreign credits took on a quite modern aspect, and this organization of commerce made possible the remarkable luxury trade of Rome. A single dinner might, and did, call for food and wine from the length of the Mediterranean and the breadth of the Alps, and a Roman mosaic was made of stones from a score of lands.

But one aspect of foreign trade was unfortunate. Goods were imported from the Far East, Cathay and the Indies. Silk for milady's gown was worth its weight

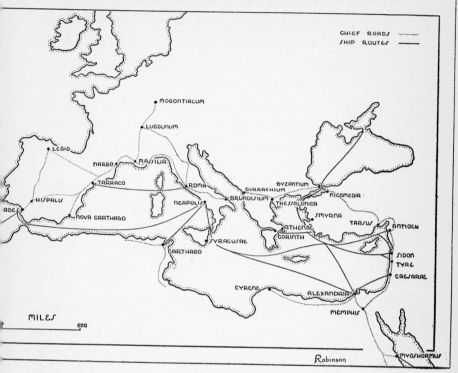

Fig. 18. Some of the main land and sea routes of the Roman Empire.

in gold on the Roman market, and these far eastern goods were paid for in bullion, a drain on Rome's economics. Rome produced nothing locally, yet she called upon her scattered provinces for necessities and luxuries, and for ideas. For export she had nothing but political services. London, Paris and Washington are much the same today. In short, Rome no longer had that provincial character in which environmentalists so delight.

As Rome became more complicated through its expanding commercial geography, as exotic commodities were multiplied, so also did Roman culture become more cosmopolitan. Every province contributed elements to the civilization of the Imperial City. The crude Britains marching into the city brought with them knowledge of forest customs; the Egyptian merchant contributed the elements of Hellenism. So complex and diverse were these contributions that only volumes could do them justice. Let us merely suggest the contributions of two areas.

Though Spain contributed one of the greatest trade volumes to Rome (more Roman coins are found in Spain than in any other province), Greece offered the finest elements of civilization. The Greek tutor or physician brought the highest prices in the slave market. From the Greeks Rome derived their stoic and epicurean philosophies. The Roman patrician had a Greek background as a matter of general culture, and the sons of wealthy parents frequently received their education in Greek schools. Rome was filled with Greek antiques and works of art. This influx of Greek ideas was partly due to the strength of that ancient culture, but its flow was kept alive by the active commerce with Greece, not so much because of Roman purchases of Greek marbles, as for the products of

Greek workshops: fine woolens, excellent metal work, wines, perfumes and medicinal herbs.

A second set of influences came from the old Fertile Crescent. Long established trade in carpets, cloth stuffs and the things that men at the edge of deserts manufacture, was partly the basis for an exchange of ideas, but also Roman governors and lesser officials returning to Rome brought home eastern ideas. In addition easterners of rank visited Rome. The East had a lavishness and luxury of life that appealed, and the sumptuousness of decadent Rome was largely due to the oriental influence. This element was in turn partly responsible for the undermining of Roman political and family morals, a direct example of culture diffusion due to imperialism.

When Alexander carried Greek conquest into the East he was, in turn, affected by an eastern concept. His father, Philip, was little more than a chieftain chosen leader of the mountain tribes. Further, ideas of democracy must have been trained into Alexander by contact with the Greek cities. But when he went into the East he found that a ruler must be a sun-god, omnipotent. Naturally, he took to the idea. It may well have been contact with the East that led the half-mad, dissolute emperors of Rome to crown themselves with wreaths.

* * * * *

Now the British Empire is of another time. Culture was so different at the opening of the seventeenth century from that at the beginning of the Christian era that the cosmopolitanism of the two is hardly comparable. Yet certain fundamentals are the same. Both empires were accidents of history. A decreasing food supply and an increasing population were shared by both.

England before Elizabeth was, as Shakespeare said, "that uttermost corner of the West." Englishmen did not voyage. Hanseatic and Venetian ships carried England's foreign commerce. The Renaissance, the Reformation, and over-population were all factors in putting Englishmen on the sea. Henry VIII and Elizabeth were both conscious of the importance of the commercial revolution and urged it on. Suddenly Englishmen broke their provincial bounds. Drake's *Golden Hind* actually encircled the world, and the most provincial country of western Europe began to receive an influx of foreign commodities and foreign ideas. An example of the importance of one material introduction is to be found in cloth. The English exchanged their woolens for cheaper cottons and for silk. Cotton was made up with linen, and the cheapness of the new stuffs promoted the use of underwear. Incidentally, the bath became an amenity of court life, and there was a measure of sanitation for the lower classes.

A number of new foods were introduced. The potato was to become the most important. At first it was grown as a curiosity, and did not strike the popular fancy because it was alleged to be dangerous. Probably Sir John Hawkins brought the potato from America to England in 1565, but certainly Sir Walter Raleigh did the same in 1580. The tomato came to the old world about the same time. One of the most important novelties was sugar. Small amounts had previously come from Sicily, but now the West Indian planters began shipping great amounts to Europe. At first it was largely used as a medicine, and over three hundred drugs had a sugar base. It was also used to preserve fruits. Then,

> *"If sugar can preserve both pears and plums,*
> *Why can it not preserve as well our lungs?"*

Soon it was so common a food and sweetmeat that people's teeth turned black from its use.

Many new flowers from seeds and bulbs were brought home by the ships. Persia, China and the Levant contributed their quota. Daffodils, tulips, and the Persian iris were among the first flowery strangers. Tropical plants forced upon England the household conservatory, so important to the Victorian romances. America sent the sunflower, the violet, Canadian lilies and many others. New trees made their appearance; the Aleppo pine, the cedar of Lebanon, the hazel nut and horse chestnut came from the Levant. Persia contributed the walnut tree, and China the white mulberry. America gave juniper, a cypress, the scarlet oak, red mulberry, black walnut, white hickory and the butternut tree.

Coffee played an unexpected role in English intellectual life. First, it freed the English from paying the Spanish and Portuguese for wines. Second, coffee became fashionable. Coffee houses (the first in 1650) were common, essentially club houses where men gathered to discuss politics, literature and art, a forum for the interchange of ideas.

Previous to the coffee habit, men had learned to smoke. John Hawkins may well lay claim to the introduction of tobacco, though Sir Walter Raleigh was the man to make it popular, for he entertained his friends with pipes and mugs of ale spiced with nutmeg. By 1614 it was reputed that there were seven thousand tobacco shops in London. Shortly tobacco became almost a necessity as a social art for both men and women. Medical properties were ascribed to it, and during the plague of 1665 people chewed and smoked it to ward off illness.

England, largely by robbing the Spaniards, obtained metals in excess of the needs of industry, so metals were used for decorative and ornamental purposes. The manufacture of silver and gold plates for table use became common. Even the middle classes had silver plate. It was even used in the kitchen. Paintings of this time show finger rings and earrings, ideas derived from Asiatic contacts. Both Sir Walter Raleigh and Charles I wore earrings. Precious stones and pearls were brought from the Indies; Elizabeth was a bejeweled queen.

New scenes, strange countries and hitherto unheard of sights stimulated the imagination of the English. Among the many effects of this was a hastened interest in science and nature study. Meteorology and oceanography had their English beginnings at this time. Many journals of voyages enriched the literature, and foreign contacts colored imagery and vocabulary. From the Dutch sailors came such words as "avast, boom, dock, hull, shipper, sloop, schooner, smuggle and lubber." Many Oriental words were taken from the Portuguese: "albatross, caste, tank, peon and port." From the Spaniards were acquired words like "buffalo, cigar, alligator, vanilla, negro and mustang." From the American Indians via the Spaniards came "barbecue, maize, canoe, hurricane, chocolate, tomato" and many others. From the Indians direct came "hickory, hominy, moose, moccasin and wigwam." Asiatic influence is to be noted in the words "mohair, coffee, henna, harem, divan, caravan, bazaar, calico, amuck, and bamboo."

These strange words and the stranger products and ideas for which they stood immensely liberated English thought. Pictures of exotic lands and races, adventurous seas and harbors, developed new interests. In the end curiosity became scientific thought. Medieval notions, ancient cosmography, and sailors' legends gave way before actual and rational investigation. The new commercialism increased standards of living in England, leading to a lavishness and indulgence never before known on the island.

So the sheer force of fact conquered the simple philosophy of the influence of local environment. It must be remembered, then, that man can enlarge his environmental contacts. More than this, man can by his choice use his environments in many different ways.

Chapter Ten

AN EXAMPLE OF

HUMAN ADJUSTMENT

MOST FACTS OF GEOGRAPHY OR OF GEOGRAPHIC IM-
plication, are not environmentalistic. Most cultural
events are quite the choice of men. This is cultural
geography.* This chapter is the story of man's choice,
the story of the beginning of western civilization in the
manner of life of the invaders and destroyers of the
Roman Empire. The steps in this rebuilding are
marked by a series of institutions, man-conceived methods by which to live. Though suggested by the mind

* See the excellent description of cultural geography in the
"Encyclopedia of Social Science," written by C. O. Sauer.

of man rather than by the environmental set-up, they all had geographic implications or functions. Such institutions were feudalism, certain works of monasticism, pilgrimages, fairs, the growth of towns, guilds, and the Crusades. Only once shall we leave cultural geography and return to environmentalism in this chapter, when we study energizing climate and its effect upon the man of the Renaissance.

With the downfall of the Roman Empire much tradition and experience in the arts of civilization was thrust aside; the barbarians set back the clock. This is the "impact" of culture, purely human interference, the Z tendency of our cube. Because of this it was necessary to go through the painful process of rebuilding civilization, which took a thousand years. This rebuilding of the edifice was, in terms of the philosophy of geography, a readaptation of environmental resources, accomplished by a series of social and economic institutions. These had certain characters which were Roman, but also they were colored distinctly by the barbarian tradition and barbarian psychology. The story has often been told by historians, but seldom has the medieval drama been presented with emphasis upon the stage setting.

Too often the setting of the human drama in any century has been presented by historians only by implication. Never in a history is there adequate description of the dark forests in which the story of early medieval Europe was enacted. There was a land of trees, in which clearings were like remote islands. The trees themselves were huge, spreading over great areas. The soft mulch of leaves frequently became forest swamp, making travel most difficult. At the time of Alfred, one-third of Saxon England was such a swamp. The scene painter for a Wagnerian opera will do better in picturing this sylvan milieu than the formal historian. The rise of medieval civilization in western Europe had the forest solitude and the individualism of forest (feudal) dwellers as its chief obstacles. One way to look at the Middle Ages is in terms of conquest of the forest.

So far history has been sun-lit. The only forests in the regions we have studied were those of the mountains, and even the mountains, by later Roman times, had been seriously deforested. The Romans, with audacity, were not satisfied to conquer only the Mediterranean basin. They crossed the Alps and took control of the forest lands in Austria, Germany, Belgium, Britain and France. Adaptation of this land called for a new technique. Road-building, settlement-making, provision against inclement weather, and agriculture all demanded new methods of life. Moreover, Roman law had to meet new problems in the strange physical environment as well as in the strange cultural tradition of the Northmen. One can expect, then, a weaker hold on the northern provinces than upon those with familiar Mediterranean conditions. A nation limited by a climatic boundary has a certain native strength, so the possession of forest provinces which were extra-Mediterranean was a critical weakness in the Roman set-up.

The first invaders were the Huns, nomads from the Russian and Siberian steppes. For a long period the Huns so pressed against the eastern borders that Constantine moved his capital from Rome to old Byzantium (Constantinople) in order to be nearer the scene of action. What caused the Huns to leave their steppe lands is not known. Probably it was a failure of grass for their herds. In any case, the Huns cut a swathe of destruction through the empire. At the German borders there lived tribes that were most war-like. Urged on by attacks from the rear, or attracted by the wealth and military weakness of the empire the Germans moved south and to the east, in a slow, gradual trek. The forest peoples began taking over Roman towns and estates. Ostrogoths, Visigoths, Burgundians, Vandals, Angles, Saxons, Jutes, Germanii, Lombards and later Franks marched into the Roman empire. When the end came, the empire did not fall, it crumbled.

The invaders of Italy came in contact with a superior culture. The barbarians took over villas and estates, and were not unwelcome. The Roman slaves and *nexi* (debtors) preferred their new masters. They did not destroy the powerful Roman civilization, but rather they took on Roman forms of life. Though decadent, Roman civilization in Italy continued, so Rome has a continuous history from the year 1000 B.C. to the present day.

Generally speaking, Romanization decreased as the distance from Rome increased. Moreover, Roman culture in the forested north existed only along the paved highways, and in a few towns and camps. The wide countryside was as yet virgin forest. Only in scattered locations did agriculture represent Roman standards. Agricultural, industrial and commercial beginnings were easily thrust aside by the barbarians, and the lands north of the Alps returned to a primitive state. The invaders had a hunting culture and were barely in the Iron Age. They absorbed little of Roman organization, and preferred their mud-walled camps and wattle or log buildings to the well-ordered Roman settlements. Roads and bridges fell into decay. Agriculture did not interest them. The invaders were well-fortified by forest isolation, and resisted most Roman cultural influences.

The Arthurian tales give us a good history of the time, but they must, of course, be divested of stone castles, armored knights and ladies living in luxury. The tales of Arthur were not composed until the eleventh century, and the heroes were clothed, armored and housed in eleventh-century equipment. Siegfried forging his sword in a forest clearing is more authentic. Arthur typifies the Celtic king, Christianized through contact with the Romans, who struggled against pagan injustice and darkness, and we know that in the long run the Christian knights lost the struggle, and Christian ideas were not reintroduced for centuries.

Out of this chaos emerged an interesting people, the Franks. As war-like as any, primitive in food and shelter habits, they yet had some sense of political organization. It was they, roaring battle cries and led by Charles, the Hammer, who hurled themselves against the Saracens at Poitiers in northern France to save western Europe for a Teutonic civilization. Their first great king was Charlemagne, crowned in 800, who came to control western Germany, Belgium and France, a vast empire of forest without means of centralization of authority. This caused the evolution of the feudal system.

The feudal system was suggested to the barbarians by a Roman tradition, but its strong hold on the north was due to a geographic condition. In short, it withstood the environmental test. At the close of Roman domination, the small farmer had become a slave to debt. To make the farmer pay his debt he was forced to remain on his land, the beginning of serfdom. That the feudal system so fastened on the north lands was due to poor communication. (This is an example of an environmental screen previously mentioned.) A king gave almost complete control of an area to a duke, who, in turn, assigned power to counts. Each community lived to itself and therefore had to govern itself. In return for services, supplies and taxes paid by the serfs, the overlords offered protection from marauding bands. Furthermore, power vested in the local lords was necessary because forest isolation prevented centralized kingly authority. Indeed, the words *wald* (forest) and *mark* (boundary) had much the same connotation. Forests in Europe have always been boundaries, down to the first World War struggle in the Argonne.

The feudal period, however, spelled cultural stagnation. The lords held their authority according to the isolation of the fiefs. It was therefore logical that they should take no steps to reduce that isolation. Commerce in commodities and commerce in ideas was almost completely lacking. Travel in the forests between clearings was dangerous. Men lived within the resources and mental limitations of one place.

An institution which broke a trail for civilization through the dark forest was monasticism. Life in those days was strife, except within the church. There security was possible, and enough of the teachings of Jesus remained to encourage asceticism. Hence the rapid growth of monasteries. The little Greek and Roman culture that survived in northwest Europe was preserved by the monks. They most nearly approached literacy. They copied pagan manuscripts, and they rendered yet a greater service by preserving and disseminating agricultural knowledge. With them work had an inherent virtue. The harder the task, the greater the glory before God. This led them to take the stony field, the steep hillside or the swamp, clear the field, terrace the hill, drain the swamp, and then with intelligence proceed to farm. They took the worst spots in western Europe and made them bloom like a rose. Monasteries in Italy stood upon terraced hills. Westminster Abbey was founded in a terrible swamp called Thorney.

The monks practiced rotation of crops, seed selection, cattle breeding and plant grafting. One monastic holding had 3000 draft oxen. And the monks were artisans, forge workers, leather workers and cloth makers, as well. Civilization recommenced.

The church also broke down the feudal ignorance of other lands, having absorbed the pagan idea that virtue lay in holy places rather than in one's own spirit. So people went on pilgrimages. Though at first the palmers were moved by sincere devotion, many later made the grand tour just for the ride. Foreign lands were no longer homes of ogres and beasties. The clerics and monks were equipped to write the travel diaries. The good fathers sometimes spun some broad tales because they were men, even as we. One itinerary has been called systematic nonsense; a good father reported a volcano that erupted on Thursdays and Saturdays!

How ignorant the early medieval geographers were is surprising in light of the progress of the Greek and Roman cartographers. Dark Age maps were based largely upon Deuteronomy and Isaiah. Maps were square because the Bible speaks of the four corners of the earth. Others were oval because of the "circuit of the earth." Jerusalem was in the center because Jerusalem was set amidst cities. The edges of the maps might show the mythical lands of Gog and Magog or even Paradise. But pilgrimages and travels overcame this darkness. Roads were improved. The monasteries took care of wayfarers and learned much from their guests. Men began to travel beyond their forest clearings, and the tiny provincial bonds were broken.

The forests for a time restricted commerce. The feudal lord policed his clearing, but the forests harbored brigands. And there was a more systematic form of robbery of the merchant caravans. Tolls were collected by the overlords to maintain their highways, but the money was seldom used for that purpose. Tolls were collected whether you went over a bridge or under it. These were the days of the robber barons of the Rhine. Seventy-four toll stations stifled traffic on the Loire. This over-taxation of commerce was the result of the land psychology of feudalism. But commerce will not be downed. In the long run the need of trade broke down the isolation of the forest clearings and created the exchange of commodities and ideas so essential to civilization.

A combination of commerce and monastic life further broke down isolation through the medium of fairs. The only time when one could find large numbers of people gathered together was during a religious festival. What more natural than that merchants should establish a bazaar before the doors of the abbey? What more natural than that poor abbeys should acquire the bone of a saint (some saints seem to have had several complete skeletons) to invite a pilgrimage and thus be able to sell space to merchants for their booths? The churches grew rich. The clearing in the forest before the doors of the abbey can be seen today in the *place* before the abbey where we stand to admire the abbey towers. The great religious feast days had the greatest fairs. Then merchants in appropriate towns gained permission from the overlord for a fair in that town. Some fairs became international, because of their situation on a great trade route or because of clever management and publicity.

After the Middle Ages, during which man strove blindly towards better living though the worst barrier to progress was man himself, there came a sudden change for the better. The Middle Ages watched the plant of civilization developing its roots; the Renaissance was the period of flowering. Still man's choice was the dominant factor, yet in this flowering we must turn for complete explanation to an environmentalistic condition, the change of climate.

It is always a good thing to jar people from habits of thinking. Indeed, it is frequently an intellectual thing to be out of step with the company. To walk up a lonely lane is to make discoveries—or get lost. The individual thinker is clever—or a fool. Most writers on the Renaissance give you Giotto as an influence on later art, tell you of the importance of the Medicis' patronage, point a finger at Michelangelo, and feel that they have gotten at the true causes of the Renaissance. I shall not do so. Leaders are made, not born. Given a certain degree of mentality, they are the result of circumstances which sweep them along to prominence. Consider the French revolution. A mob dashes past a café. One man rushes after them, shouting to his astonished comrades, "I must hurry, I'm the leader!" A leader senses where the crowd is going and dashes on ahead. John Huss walked alone and was seized upon and burned. Luther was astonished to find that because he uttered protests against the established church, he was swept up and carried to fame by a multitude of whose number he was only faintly aware.

What were the tendencies of the times which found so many leaders, artists and writers, in Italy in the fourteenth and fifteenth century? Was there suddenly a flood of temperamental mutations in human evolution? One doubts it, though there were some. Certain men of genius hastened the embellishment of the human mind which we call the Rebirth. Dante was one of these. One student expressed this well, though with unconscious humor, when he wrote, "Dante stood with one foot firmly implanted in the Middle Ages while with the other he waved a greeting to the new dawn of the Renaissance."

The early Middle Ages were feudal, futile, unsanitary and stagnating. Hope for progress in civilization lay in the middle class, the merchants and artisans. Except for a few fat burghers with better houses, the middle class lived in towns amidst smells, walled in by fortifications. Those were the thousand years without a bath!

Finally, a single purpose prevailed in the isolated manors and fiefs scattered over western Europe. This purpose was a genuine intolerance, a desire for bigger and better fighting, and a hope for booty. We call the result the Crusades. I suspect that the Italian cities sent lobbyists to the Pope to urge this holy purpose, and *how* the delegates must have rubbed their hands and gloated over the prospect of business. The Crusades were just that; they broke down a penny-wise economy and substituted big business. Athens gave us democratic practices; Rome gave us legal habits, but Venice gave us modern business practices, funded debts, public banks and money.

Venice, Florence, Genoa and Marseilles made their fortunes in those days of capital investments, fat dividends, inventories, orderliness and system. And there was *no* income tax!! People had wealth and to spare. Today the rich occupy their time in building to salve their consciences. Some build cathedrals, some give money for college buildings which will bear their name, and some, the high fliers, buy immortality by patronizing the arts. There is today and there was in the Middle Ages a very definite relationship between big business, surplus profits and art.

If the Crusades encouraged big business, they also promoted travel, improving roads and inns, and creating such conveniences as letters of credit. They shattered the provincial casing on the collective provincial mind, and became one of the greatest agencies of culture-diffusion on record. Food for thought was developed by the two main contacts the Crusaders established in the East.

The first was Constantinople, the treasure house of Byzantine culture. All through the Dark Ages Constantinople, behind most splendid fortifications, preserved the Graeco-Roman civilization known to us as Byzantine. Constantinople, from the point of view of embellished culture, was the only real European center of civilization of the period. You will remember how the armies of the fourth Crusade took Constantinople, which makes one doubt their true religious purpose. It is said that the scholars of that city seized their manuscripts and the artists took their brushes and hied themselves to Italy. Success attracts art, always.

The second contact was with the Muslim world, the direct heir to Egypt, Babylonia, Persia and an eastern form of Hellenism. Indeed, parts of Aristotle were preserved for us in a Christian monastery in Bagdad. We westerners have little conception of the glory of the Muslim Empire, for it extended from India to the Atlantic. Bagdad controlled cities as far east as Samarcand. Damascus was then at the height of its glory. Cairo was a second capital. Kairowan was a revival of Carthage. Fez, in northwestern Africa, was another great Muslim center, and Seville, Cordoba, Granada and Toledo stood for the glory of Muslim Spain. These Muslims were cultivated gentlemen compared with our feudal lords, the houses of the rich were magnificent,

their universities taught alchemy, algebra,* medicine
and philosophy, they had a fine sense of justice and
definitely an intellectual way of life. Also the Muslims
had a curious habit, for though water was at a pre-
mium in the desert they bathed. Theirs were the ideas
that irrigated Europe, especially Italy.

The story of the Muslims in Europe becomes a lesson
in the diffusion of culture. Fine manners came through
their commerce with the Muslims, and the peak of
fine manners is intellectuality and creative art. So far,
great wealth and contact with other civilizations have
been postulated as aids in the development of the
Renaissance, but we must search for more dominating
factors for the concentration of the Renaissance in
Venetia and the Lombard towns. In short, *why* did the
Renaissance occur in Italy? We know the historian's
explanation of commercial contacts. Was there any reason yet more geographic?

The best path is not always the shortest, so pardon
what may seem to be digression. Some climates are
more energizing than others. Every city worthy the
name in the United States has a Chamber of Commerce, societies for the promotion of this and for the
prevention of that. Columbus, Ohio, for example, has
two Chambers of Commerce. When, on the other hand,
one finds a Chamber of Commerce in Georgia, it represents human initiative at work in spite of the lassitude
imposed by a less various weather.

* Words with the prefix "al" as "alcohol" are Arabic.

What is now to be said is taken directly from the researches of a most suggestive geographer and environmentalist, Ellsworth Huntington, who has proved all this statistically.* He says that certain variability of

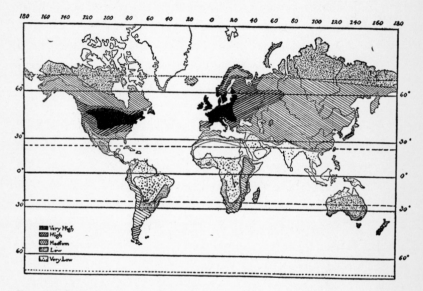

Fig. 19. The distribution of climatic energy. After Ellsworth Huntington, "Civilization and Climate." The Yale University Press.

weather promotes energy. Generally, the range of weather elements is slightly lower for mental energy than for the physical. The examination grades at West Point and Annapolis show a direct response to barometric pressure, temperature and the like. Errors in

* Ellsworth Huntington, "Civilization and Climate," "World Power and Evolution," and numerous other contributions.

New York banks increase in hot spells. Physical energy is best measured by piece work in factories. Huntington mapped the zones of climatic energy according to statistical representation. Then he asked philosophers the

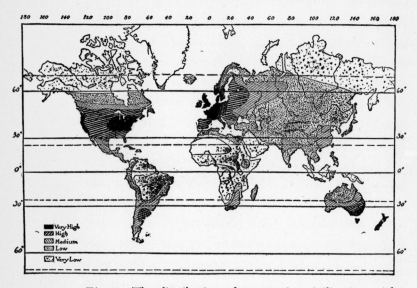

Fig. 20. The distribution of progressive civilizations. After Ellsworth Huntington, "Civilization and Climate." The Yale University Press.

world around to map civilization zones according to their progressiveness. The two maps, which are here reproduced, coincide to a remarkable degree. There are then zones of energy and zones of lassitude.

It is Huntington's theory that the climate of centuries preceding the fourteenth was in northern Europe highly conducive to progress. The cathedral building

of the thirteenth century bears witness. But the century
that preceded the Renaissance was another matter. In
this period the ice drift cut off communication with
Greenland, and the advancing glaciers almost literally
pushed the settlements into the sea. Crops failed in
Norway and then in England and France. A great
cold wave was experienced from 1313 to 1324. There
was, also, too much rain. The Caspian Sea expanded;
and the tree rings in California ran to an excessive
width. Horses and men crossed the frozen Baltic on
foot. The Rhine, Danube, and the Thames froze.
Fifty-five summers of the century saw violent floods,
and the cathedral at Mayence was submerged to the
famous frieze over the door. There were nineteen un-
paralleled storms on the Baltic. In the Netherlands
seventy-two villages were destroyed in one night,
200,000 people were drowned in one year. There were
famines in 1315, 1316, 1321, 1351 and 1369. The Black
Death, Asiatic cholera, the Athenian plague and famine
killed 13,000,000 people in China, and reduced the population of France and England by one-third. This is
not all of the calamity, but let us come up for breath.
We do not know the cause of all this, but we know that
variability of weather increases in ratio to the number
of sunspots. Those ancient astronomers, the Chinese,
said the fourteenth century had excessive sunspots.

Now back to the Lombard towns. If in the north the
belt of excessive variability expanded until weathers
overwhelmed civilization and almost caused a return

of glacial ice, there must have been a belt farther south where a lesser variability was just sufficient for progress in civilization. Well, Dante wrote "The Divine Comedy" between the years 1300 and 1310. Along came Giovanni, Andrea Pisano, Giotto, Fra Angelico and Botticelli. Leonardo da Vinci and Michelangelo, in the fifteenth century, had the advantage of an energizing climate as well as the precedent of the genius of the fourteenth century. Leonardo said, "All the genius that I have comes from the air (climate) of my native province." He had so much energy that he is noted as a geologist and engineer, and he made an independent invention of the wheelbarrow. The Medicis were a Chamber of Commerce in themselves, and from Machiavelli came a handbook on the promotion of misgained wealth, "The Prince." Now, heaven forbid that anyone should explain genius by climate, but it is my theory that genius in Italy today (excepting our energetic mutant, Mussolini) sits in the sun and basks. After a month at Taormina I found myself getting out early so as to be sure of a seat in the sun on the marble benches about the cathedral.

And so the Italian Renaissance was the logical consequence of the commercial contacts with Lombardy in particular, and with the Byzantine and Muslim worlds. Artistic expression was supported by the wealth of this same trade. But this stimulation to business, to art and to ideas came in no small part from an energizing climate. It was said earlier in this manuscript that if the climate remained passive, the deterministic point of view could hardly be maintained, but, that if climate shifted, facts might be plotted close to the corner B on our oft-referred-to cube. Energizing climate, if we accept the facts, certainly approaches determinism. Yet one must remember that most of the stages in recivilizing the western world after the barbarian debacle were definitely man's choice, and should come under the head of cultural geography.

Chapter Eleven

APPROXIMATIONS TO

REGIONAL PSYCHOLOGY

Now THAT WE HAVE PASSED THE RENAISSANCE AND find ourselves in full bloom, we have arrived in the enlightened modern period. It is true there are to develop such blights upon our blossom as the Industrial Revolution, the Crimean Campaign, the *Raft of the Medusa,* and the First and Second Opium Wars. But, except for these purple spots on our lily-white flower of progress, we are moving onward and upward towards that acme of cultural and scientific advancement known as the First World War. In order to understand how millions of men in hog-like gas masks came to believe sincerely that they were fighting for principle, even for the tenets of the gentle Jesus, while men on the opposite side were calling upon that same Jesus for victory, we must explain the manner by which men could arrive at such opposing points of view. It cannot be that because one people had iron and another coal, that one had colonies and another not, that men should fight. Belgium has meager resources, and dense population, yet she does not offer to fight. Racial likes and dislikes represent attitudes of mind. I do not understand why my Italian barber was taught to hate the Austrians in the third grade and the French in the fifth grade. But if we must write upon provincial conflicts, are we to be permitted to ignore completely the most characteristic aspect, that of regional psychology?

Geographers do not scorn psychology. Rather it is that geographers are, strange to say, so disdainful of environmentalism that that most interesting study is falling into the hands of psychologists, sociologists and others. Psychologists have much to contribute to environmentalism. They have, for example, coined the phrase "behavioral environment," an acknowledgment that environment is real to us only in what we conceive it to be. "What is real is what has effects." A man unknowingly crosses a frozen lake disguised by a snow cover. He does so fearlessly, only to die of fright when told what he did. His behavioral environment was based upon his concept of safety. The psychologist, however, uses the term "environment" more inclusively than does your present writer. Psychological environment is the totality of conditions past and present, physical, social, and behavioral, which lead up to a response.

All individuals have not the same imaginative ability. Why cannot isolated groups have a common direction of mental evolution? There is nothing environmental in mental characteristics, or is there? So we come to the question of race. Is there a Celtic imagination as such? Was Roman thoroughness a racial characteristic? Were Assyrian babies cruel from birth? Or are mental characteristics merely cultural habits?

Though I know about mutants, I do not believe greatly in differences in racial mental characteristics. There is, in reality, no such thing as racial purity. Nobody is less pure ethnically than the northern Italian. The Bavarian is not a north German, and the Prussian is a mixture of heaven knows how many bloods, and I suspect the Jews have more religious solidarity than ethnic unity. In fifty generations we have 1,000,000,-000,000,000 ancestors. What mongrels we be! Or, rather, how normal we all are! With so many ancestral components we can hope to be little more than average. Certainly race could hardly be expected to show differentiation from the average. Only the divergent individual can evidence genius. Of course, thus far we have been talking about inherent mental capacity. Intelligence is not exactly coincidental with mental capacity; it is largely healthy gray matter plus training. Since we are on the average *only* average, intelligence must be training. J. B. Watson * has said that if he is given a dozen healthy, well-formed infants, *and* given his own specified environments, he can make any one of the infants a doctor, lawyer, merchant, or thief.

I find myself not so far from Watson's statement. Mind is little if it is not exercised. My university was visited by the second fastest lightning calculator in the world. The psychologists said this was defeat, and proceeded to turn him into the first lightning calculator. They then took the janitor and started *him* on the way towards rapid calculating until forced to give up because of the dust on the floors. It is not gray matter that sets the limitations so much as our limited knowledge of mental processes.

In short, we are what we are because, due to earlier circumstances, we have had no choice. Most babies are savages that have not yet responded to the stimuli of the local milieu. A baby born on a South Sea island but taken from its parents to be raised on the sidewalks of New York does not begin to dream of moon-lit coral islands at maturity. Jack London was more romantic than right when he wrote the "Call of the Wild." With a few exceptions, we all start remarkably equal. The human record at birth, except for instincts, is blank.

Though races of men have an average inherent mental capacity, they do not have the same intelligence. Intelligence is the capacity to enlarge the significance of the environment. It is also true that problems of

* "Behaviorism."

environment enlarge intelligence. Porteus, a psychologist, thinks the naked Bushman of South Africa has considerable intelligence because he lives in a land of meager resources and needs intelligence for existence. Our intelligentsia, Porteus implies, is *very* unintelligent because of its easy surroundings. Do you remember the story of the noble lady of France who won the applause of her guests because she had intelligence enough to open the folding doors to her dining room all by herself? The lady did not lack gray matter; she and her kind had never been trained to open doors. And long ago we decided that intelligence was not inherited. What is "inherited" is really acquired. Habits of a psychological nature are as much culture as political ideas or systems of crop rotation. Any holdover of cultural forms from one generation to another is due to the persisting influence of environment.

The quality of intelligence, that is, a people's temperamental attitude toward life, is the ultimate measure of provincialism. It is not enough to know whether people eat wheat or rice. If they are well-fed, the materials are of slight importance. Moreover, it is the quality of life rather than the quantity that is significant. One may know a people better through their art and literature than through their artichokes and legumes. Granted that people have differing psychologic qualities, but are these any concern of the environmentalist? Let me put the question in another fashion. Is there any psychological response to the physical milieu to be found in the works of Thomas Hardy, Willa Cather, Louis Adamic, Hamlin Garland and a thousand others? For a grand example of physical circumstance influencing the quality of men study Pearl Buck's hero in "The Good Earth." Another classic for this is "Ethan Frome" by Edith Wharton. Mrs. Wharton painted the dreariness of a New England winter and then drew her characters against it in the same gray tone. One passage from the book runs: "About a mile farther, on a road I had never traveled, we came to an orchard of starved apple trees writhing over a hillside among outcroppings of slate that nuzzled up through the snow like animals pushing out their noses to breathe. Beyond the orchard lay a field or two, their boundaries lost under drifts; and above the fields, huddled against the white immensities of land and sky, one of those lonely New England farmhouses that make the landscape lonelier." This is the preface to a great human drama.

However, one must be cautious in ascribing psychological qualities to environment. I hesitate to qualify remarks made by so great a stylist as Virginia Woolf, and yet her delightful explanation in "Orlando" of Victorianism is more fun than fact. I quote at length, for it is too good to miss:

"This great cloud which hung, not only over London, but over the whole of the British Isles on the first day of the nineteenth century, stayed long enough to have extraordinary consequence upon those who lived beneath its shadow. A change seemed to have come over the climate of England. Rain fell frequently, but only in fitful gusts, which were no sooner over than they began again. But what was worse, damp now began to make its way into every house—damp, which is the most insidious of all enemies, for while the sun can be shut out by blinds, and the frost roasted by a hot fire, damp steals in while we sleep; damp is silent, imperceptible, ubiquitous.

"Thus, stealthily, and imperceptibly, none marking the exact day or hour of the change, the constitution of England was altered and nobody knew it. Everywhere the effects were felt. The hardy country gentleman, who had sat down gladly to a meal of ale and beef in a room designed perhaps by the brothers Adam, with classic dignity, now felt chilly. Rugs appeared, beards were grown and trousers fastened tight under the instep. The chill which he felt in his legs he soon transferred to his house; furniture was muffled; walls and tables were covered, too. Then a change of diet became essential. The muffin was invented and the crumpet. Coffee supplanted the after-dinner port, and, as coffee led to a drawing-room in which to drink it, and a drawing-room to glass cases, the glass cases to artificial flowers, and artificial flowers to mantelpieces, and mantelpieces to pianofortes, and pianofortes to drawing-room ballads (skipping a stage or two) to innumerable little dogs, mats, and antimacassars, the home—which had become extremely important—was completely altered.

"The damp struck within. Men felt the chill in their hearts; the damp in their minds. In a desperate effort to snuggle their feelings into some sort of warmth one subterfuge was tried after another. Love, birth, and death were all swaddled in a variety of fine phrases. The sexes drew further and further apart. No open conversation was tolerated. Evasions and concealments were sedulously practiced on both sides."

O. E. Baker is a philosophical farm economist in Washington. He analyzes the quality of mind in a more convincing, though less amusing fashion than Mrs. Woolf. He says agricultural life in America makes for a greater complexity of thinking processes than the herding or collectional cultures, more leisure for arts, crafts and philosophies, permanent homes which are at once storehouses for foods and ideologies, and a greater sense of organization and planning. Baker's remarks justify the study of regional psychology.

What we have said so far is only that people's minds in certain cases do react to environment. Racial mental qualities are different more or less as the habitats are different. Ellsworth Huntington is the best defender of this thesis.* Porteus comes to the same conclusion after laboratory investigations. MacDougall, in "The Group Mind," says that "physical environment affects the mental qualities of a people in three manners; firstly, it directly influences the mind of each generation; secondly, it moulds the mental constitution by natural

* See his "The Character of Races."

selection, adapting the race to itself; thirdly, it exerts indirect influence by determining the occupations and modes of life, and through these, the social organization of a people."

MacDougall elaborates these points. He uses climate as an illustrative factor, mentioning temperature and moisture as determinatives. His interesting argument informs the reader that there is a strong possibility that mental qualities are affected through the influence of bodily habits, the senses, and the imagination, upon the mind. He concludes his remarks by saying that physical factors mold the acquired characters but that there is not sufficient evidence to show that "the acquired characters so induced ever become innate or racial characters by direct transmission." Recognizing the importance of the immediate environment, we exclude ourselves from the possibility of proving mental characters as innate. Biologists will agree with this, and, anyway, man is too sensitive an agent of expression of his milieu for so frail a possible inheritance to endure.

Though we are in no way preaching the evolution of mental characteristics as acquired traits, it is constantly necessary to refute the idea. William James says, "No geographical environment can produce a given type of mind; it can only foster and further certain types ... and thwart and frustrate others." But the mental habits of one generation are inherited through the persistence of culture by the next generation. In this way races, groups, or nations "inherit" cultural char-

acters and so achieve a different quality of mind. Whole
books have been written upon the difference between the
Teuton and the Latin. Since the barbarians at the
downfall of Rome gave much Teuton or Slavic blood
to the Latin countries, one wonders if isolation from
each other, combined with differing geographic qualities of locale, is not responsible for the variations. Certainly there is a differing quality of mind. Could a
German have phrased the significant Italian social
axiom, "The sun is the father of ragamuffins"? Could
you expect an Italian, unless so trained, properly to
sing, "Du, du liegst mir im Herzen"?

One of the first mental characteristics one would like
to measure is imagination, which in turn leads to art,
music, invention, and cultural advance. Archibald
Geikie wrote an only partially satisfactory book upon
this subject entitled "Landscape and History." There
is, of course, a varying use of imagination according
to the temper of the times. Is there provincialism in
the quality of imagination? For years, I have written
notes upon the geography of the art, architecture, invention, and philosophy of people only to tear them up.
One set had slightly more significance than the rest;
that was upon folk music.

Music is one of the most primitive and yet most ex-
pressive of the artistic creations. Of all the arts, musical
rhythm alone is apparently sensible to animals. But in
spite of this elemental character, it expresses, as does no
other medium, tribal or racial temperaments. Musical

interpretations of that simple life which is the out-
growth of the soil are, in the nature of things, folk
music. Folk themes, begun perhaps before musical notation was invented, were transmitted through the centuries by the medium of singers. In a world often grim
and repellent, the singers preserved and passed on their
art, which, more than any save poetry, is a record of
temperament. Whereas in modern music the personality of the composer is paramount, in the past the individuality of the composer was inevitably obliterated
when the people put their own interpretations upon
the songs, instilling the spirit of the land, the climate,
and the time. Thus the color of the melodies is the true
temper of the people, and the musical themes which
we associate with this or that nation today, are likely
to be only reflections of geographic conditions. This is
more particularly true of folk songs which tell the
story of simple people who live close to the earth. The
plowing of fields, the joy of the harvest, the quiet hour
at sunset, the drifting of the hay barges along the canal,
the watching of the flocks on the high alp, these have
established the characters of the vicinal motifs. Even
in more recent intellectual works, the underlying theses
frequently possess a similarity which harks back to the
original refrains.

Let us take as an example of Latin music that of the
Spaniards. The most characteristic music of Iberia is
that of the south. The densely populated valley of the
Guadalquiver has a climate that is African. In this

scene of plenty, in the irrigated gardens beneath brilliant suns, the spirit is vivacious and nonchalant. Amid the chestnut groves sounds the castanet, made of those very trees. The inherent vitality of the region expresses itself in song and dance. Central Spain is a high plateau, bleak in winter, delightful in spring which is advent to the season of gaiety, and hot in summer, bringing in the languorous note. Thus there are two tempos commonly employed to depict Spanish life— the fast and fiery, representing nations bred under sunny skies; and the slow and sensuous, music of hot days and amorous nights.

All of these characteristics are in marked contrast to the music of Germany. Inevitably, the gay and impulsive south and the thoughtful and introspective north developed contrasting music. German music is full of the lyric tenderness and sentimental enjoyment of wooded shades, long, soft twilights, and the glow of the hearth. The compositions are serious and stately. Any artistic production from such a country would, in a natural order of things, be intellectual, and music is no exception to the rule. Their gaiety has nothing of the spontaneity of the Italians. The Teuton treats music with gravity, and aspires to indicate both concrete and abstract ideas, with the result that under him it reached an enviable development.

We may go yet farther north for greater contrast. Norway is cut off from southern influences by a high, sterile plateau which is storm-bound and snow-bound much of the year. It faces for the most part a northerly, though warm, sea and its shores are veiled with great banks of somber fog. It is a land of beautiful, lonely fiords, where there is much sublimity of landscape, and a great, continuous struggle for existence. The hunger of the back country, combined with the long wharf facing the sea, and the severity of conditions by which life is sustained, have given a peculiar coloring to the national music. There is a tendency towards minor tonalities, with the frequent introduction of a pathetic and dreamy note suggesting the listless tides upon the shore of lonely places, while through the melodies runs an undercurrent of solemnity inspired by the cold and dark of the northern winter.*

*Two standard works on folk songs are F. H. Botsford's: "Folk Songs of Many People" (See Vol. II) and H. F. Gilbert's: "One Hundred Folk Songs from Many Countries." Gilbert's title speaks of countries and Botsford's mentions people; a nice point. Try the *Skeye Boat Song* (Gilbert p. 21), *Venetian Barcarolle* (Gilbert p. 62), *The Fisherman* (Botsford p. 282). Whether Scotch, Italian or Portuguese, boat songs have much in common. These are for small boats and have none of the lustiness of the songs of the sailors on the larger boats. A typical Norwegian song in a minor key is *Kraakalund* (Botsford p. 202). For a Russian motif use *Winter* (Gilbert p. 86). For that German sentimentality born of forest shades try *Parting* (Gilbert p. 51), *Secret Love* (Botsford, p. 163), or *Three Leaves on the Linden Tree* (Botsford p. 171). The trends in Spanish folk music are shown by the languorous *Spanish Gypsy* (Gilbert p. 69), and by the festive *La Cachucha* (Gilbert p. 63).

You may not be entirely convinced that these melodies are due to contrasted environment but, in any case, they show grand provincialism. True, these are only straws in the wind, but if many straws blow the same way we may at least speak of tendencies.

One also has some success measuring racial conduct and morals. Soil, resources, climate, and the exigencies of life all reflect themselves in the question of morals. Desert men steal, and necessity justifies their acts. I went to war with desert men and they stole so freely we were compelled to counter steal. Later, in a Saharan community, my social standing was enhanced by knowing a high-class rug thief. Lombroso, in his monumental work on Crime says regions of excessive cold have a minimum of outbreaks against society. So much energy is expended in procuring food, clothing and fuel that a visionary or unstable character is the rare exception. Imagination is less active and the mind less irritable. Travelers generally ascribe to the Eskimos peaceful natures. So placid are the Eskimos that among certain tribes there is said to be no word for quarrel.

Irregularities of conduct and crime seem to increase with decreasing latitude and increasing variability of weather. An additional factor in the increase of crimes in the middle latitudes as against those in high latitudes is the density of population. There is a greater percentage of crimes per thousand people in a densely populated region than there is in one with few inhabitants. The hot Mediterranean country is supposed to excite the nerves as does alcohol. The slight necessities of food and clothing minimize the serious responsibilities of life which people of colder climates must carry. Boasting, stealing, quarreling, and outbursts of passion have

greater prevalence in Mediterranean regions than farther north, and the types of crimes differ in different
latitudes. The hot, languorous nights are more responsible for the careful guarding of women in the Latin
countries than is race or arbitrary custom. The veil of
the Mohammedan women probably has a similar explanation.

In the equatorial regions, enervated by great heat and
humidity combined, crime seems to decrease because of
the inertia of the people. Yet in more energetic regions
crimes increase with rising temperatures. But social
standards of moral conduct here, according to the white
man's standards, are low. This does not mean that there
are not naked, backward people in the jungle who have
high morals, but for the most part, particularly in
sexual matters, their life is on a different basis. Living-
stone voiced his disgust at the sexual aspects of the
minds of his black men, and Kipling contrasted English and Indian ideals of morality when he wrote:

*"And the wildest dreams of Kew are facts in Khatmandu
And the crimes of Clapham chaste in Martaban."*

What is immoral depends in part upon what is important to the people. We consider a salt tax as unjust,
but a tobacco tax is acceptable. In early America, horse
stealing was a heinous crime; it is not so today. I remember the story of an Austrian village whose support
depended upon swine culture. The people thought in
terms of swine. One man was ostracized by the group,

not simply because he stole, but because he stole the milk that belonged to little pigs.

I am not yet ready to construct a map of regional psychologies, nor will I ever be ready to do so, but that regional differences exist all will grant. Certain psychological qualities have locale even though there are no boundaries. The burden of proof that regional psychologies are, in part, a result of contrasted physical circumstances is mine. I shall find many philosophers, if not all geographers, on my side. Among them is J. B. Priestley, who in the third sentence of his so excellent travel book, "English Journey," tells how as guides to the study of English provincialism he took with him three books: Muirhead's "Blue Guide to England," Stamp and Beaver's "Geographic and Economic Survey" and the "Oxford Book of English Prose." The first two were for basic facts of provincialism, but for the interpretation of English life he turned from regional facts to regional ideas.

Divergencies of imagination may be the beginning of ideologic differences in people, but the culmination of racial antipathies has been political variances. When we consider political attitudes we discover more tangible factors in their causation. There is much realism in political theory. Governments of one sort or another may save the soul, but generally governments are economic programs. The geography in each program is a measure of the degree to which the plan is in harmony with the ecological conditions of the country. Essentially, there are two parties in any government. The conservative party believes that geographic or social adjustments extant at the moment should be preserved. The liberal group believes new adjustments should be made, and liberals are often hungry. When liberals are well-fed they become conservatives, though they often fail to change the party name. Montesquieu was one of the first to think upon the problem. He made many interesting statements, but was too much in the vanguard to be always correct. He said that despotism belongs to the plains and liberty to the mountains. Such broad generalizations are, of course, inaccurate, and yet in my pleasant research in the geography of mountain life, I did come to certain conclusions.

Perhaps no side of the political geography of mountains has been more discussed than the political attitude of mountain folk. Many of the statements are broad generalities which cannot be substantiated. Yet there are political attributes of mountaineers, which, if imponderable, nevertheless deserve discussion. Ratzel, Miss Semple, Vallaux, and Whittlesey have insisted upon the relationship between the state and soil. In mountainous country, the size of the terrain and the character of the topography, as well as the degree of relief, have been little short of deterministic in matters economic and political.

That the mountaineer by the nature of his homeland is an individualist has long been a popular theme, not without a certain justification. The unbending individualism of the feud-waging mountaineer of the Southern Appalachians would support the contention. Clans are confined to valleys, and valleys force upon their people an inbreeding, so it is the separated valley spaces rather than any blood relationships which in the last analysis are the basis of the feuds. No organization yet developed has broken down the social isolation of the mountain folk of the Balkans. The Balkans, the Scottish Highlands, and the Appalachian mountain areas are uplands maturely dissected. The social response to the character of dissection is in each case the same. Maturely dissected uplands are notorious for the feuds they engender.

On the other hand, the freedom of the mountaineer in well-populated alpine regions is a characteristic of the group rather than of the individual. In reality, the corridor character of great glaciated valleys, the communal character of the exploitation of alpine pastures, common danger from catastrophe, and the altitudinal distribution of property, force upon the people of a single valley a co-operation which creates a syndicate with republican and socialistic aspects. The people are a closely-knit social group. Alpine lands are owned in common because they cannot easily be subdivided. Forested slopes are of public interest. Avalanches must be prevented through community effort by planting, or the construction of walls. Public routes of communication are rendered useless by floods and avalanches, and must be restored by common effort. Mountain terracing means detailed regulation controlling rights of access, erosion and soil replacement. Irrigation on these terraces means the construction of a trunk canal and public regulation of the distribution of water. The sending of the cattle, sheep and goats up to a common pasture under a herdsman or a group of herdsmen increases group co-operation, and the summer cheese industry means a proportional sharing of profits.

In short, there is a group organization, political and social, based upon a common interest in the struggle against catastrophes, and in the use of resources. Nature forces upon the commune a group interest in resources, and in the exploitation of those resources. The economic "folk unity" is the basis of the political division. It has been asserted that from a sociological point of view there is no political boundary, but rather a shifting frontier. Such a statement has an element of truth for areas of the plains, but it is much less applicable to the mountain-rimmed areas. Each area which has physical definitions will support, to a greater or less degree, a group consciousness and a cultural provincialism.

One of the interesting histories of geographic thought is by Franklin Thomas.* In it he says that the state is but an organization for adjusting and controlling the conflicting interests of the citizens, or classes of citizens. What these interests will be, their relative strength, and the intensity of struggle between them will depend

* "The Environmental Basis of Society."

in large measure upon the nature of their geographical habitat. Giddings elaborates this idea, and explains that in a region of meager resources isolated from the benefits of richer terrain, there is strong but simple social organization. More favored regions have a dense population whose very density permits vast inequality of wealth, and the development of class governments. In rich, accessible environments every variety of mental difference is found. If the group is of the heterogeneous type their political theory varies with the nature, or stage of their social evolution and assimilation. If the community is made up of wholly miscellaneous elements, the prevailing social theory will be that Might makes Right. If the society has been created by invasion and conquest, there will develop the race or class conflict theory of political sovereignty. When the original conquerors weaken, so their position has to be sustained through intrigue, social theory takes on the nonspiritual cast reflected in the doctrines of Machiavelli. When social development proceeds further, so that a considerable degree of uniformity has developed in the group, there grow up the contract and legal sovereignty theories of political organization. Finally, when nearly perfect assimilation, homogeneity and a resulting consciousness of kind have been produced, there originates the highest, or the idealistic, theory of social origin and development.*

* Merriam, Barnes and Others, "Political Theories in Recent Times," pp. 263-265.

But nothing is static, and all generalizations are untrue, including this one. There is the principle of activity. Restated, this is that as culture changes and environment changes, no geographical detail can be true for more than a moment. Treitschke, the historian, calls attention to the fact that before the Industrial Revolution, the hilly northwest of England was the seat of all reaction and backwardness, but since that time it has been transformed into a section of industry and radicalism because of the discovery of coal and iron in the district. It is evident from a study of the history of political thought that tradition and ideas are constantly warring with one another. The struggle goes steadily on, and if there is any one principle that may be applied to both geographic environment and political thought, that principle is the principle of change.

The attitudes of people as to reaction or liberalism, as to war or peace, are essentially economic. It is the old question of the haves and the have-nots, and we are not yet through with the matter. But, if we have converted you to a belief in the geography of mental characteristics, then perhaps we can use the concept as a postulation in a discussion of group antipathies which culminated in the awful thunder of the first World War.

Chapter Twelve

THE MODERN ECONOMIC
REGION HAS PSYCHOLOGIC
CHARACTER

220

THE WESTERN WORLD BECAME VERY COMPLEX AFTER
the Renaissance. The fifteenth and sixteenth centuries
were marked by world-wide explorations which resulted in Europe in what is known as the Commercial
Revolution. This movement not only put foreign commerce on a grand scale, but by its cosmopolitan nature
liberated the culture of the countries which played a
part in the sea travel. Books written upon the subject
are commonly entitled "The Expansion of Europe."
Perhaps it was not the spread of European culture so
much as the expansion of life within Europe, that

marks the period as important. Be that as it may, this expansion seems to have been the result of the intellectual curiosity of the times, the demands of the new capitalism for a field of exploitation, and certainly because of over-population. As in the case of Phoenicia, or nineteenth-century Germany, the increase of maritime interest in the fifteenth and sixteenth centuries was a response to the over-population of Europe, over-population in terms of the culture of the times.

This last phrase brings us to one of the few axiomatic principles of geography. Over-population is a term which has meaning only when thought of in terms of the culture of the moment, or as we say, the state of the arts. This is true for all geographic facts. Since there are our now familiar three variables in the make-up of any geographic fact or event, the situation at any one moment is not true the next moment. Every fact is, as it were, a snapshot. This condition of change is known as the principle of activity.

There followed hard on the Commercial Revolution a dark, inhuman period known as the Industrial Revolution, which had a direct relationship to increasing populations. It was a means of using the trade in commodities brought to Europe through the new imperialism. Certain areas became highly industrialized. The localization of this industrialization depended upon the presence of some local resource, upon labor supply, upon power resources, or access to market. All of these factors have geographic implications, yet the industrial areas had less to do with the character of local landscape or climate, than did the subsistence economics of earlier periods. In short, man's voluntary choice was becoming more important. In the cube shown on an early page, facts and events, especially as we come to the seventeenth and eighteenth centuries, are to be plotted nearer to the dimension which represents human volition.

The location of manufacturing areas is a specialized subject. Involving commerce as it does, it always has extra-regional aspects. Site is henceforth a matter of extra-regional economics. Yet because the simple environmental factor becomes less dominant as we approach the modern period, geography is not finished for us as a study. Geography now becomes human ecology, physiological bionomics. Thus geography, always concerned with distribution, is called upon to explain the causal basis of "homes." It is the same rational process, but the factors differ in modern times from what they were in days of simpler economics. The essential difference between the modern geographic region and that of earlier times is that the modern region has a cultural complex which is particularly difficult to delimit as to area. Its various cultural elements are interlaced and they have ramifications with remote regionalisms. A region implies boundaries, but in the modern period for the most part one is not studying regions but locality complexes.

In the past we had a province or a region (the words are almost interchangeable) if there was a homoge-

neity of physical circumstance throughout the area, as
well as some suitable physical feature to serve as a
boundary. Thus the plain of Attica coincided with
Athenian provincialism. There, except for the sea approach, mountains stood as defenses before armies or
ideas, making themselves felt most in early morning
or late evening when they cast cool shadows over the
dusty plain. And islands are provinces, perfect provinces, bounded by the surf. Kashmir is the gorge of the
upper Indus River, and, guarded by peaks of almost
unbelievable height, the Vale is the most distinctive of
the Indian provinces. In Spanish days, before our
speedy, streamlined era, the valley of California was
also a province.

Not all regionalisms are so well-defined. More than
this, the activities of mice and men have altered what
the Creator apparently intended. The plain of Flanders
was a province. It had a soil area whose rich returns
were in part responsible for the wealth of Flemish culture. The intensive cultivation of the plain, added to
the industry of its many cities, supported a dense population, which had until modern times a true provincial
consciousness. It was an historical entity. Yet after the
creation of Belgium, one-third of Flanders was in
France and two-thirds in Belgium. In this case political
provincialism has been stronger than physical provincialism.

Modern economic regionalism has further complicated matters. We must of necessity divide the world

into areas which represent the land as man sees fit to use it. This was done for North America by the dynamic J. Russell Smith. The congress to which Smith presented his ideas refused to support him, preferring to be conservative rather than realistic. He went ahead on his own and wrote the most entertaining geography textbook we possess, called "North America." Smith divides North America into *human-use* regions. These are most rational. They take cognizance of the reciprocal relation in the definition of geography. Greater New York is a human-use region wherein the geographic boundaries are constantly changed by the dictates of man. Having deprecated the study of man's influence upon the earth, let me now confess that most geographic facts actually lie within the realm of man's influence upon the earth. This fact leads most geographers to study man's influence on the earth rather than environmentalism.

Not all human-use regions are obviously geographic, but, with certain inevitable exceptions, most of them fail to become permanent if they have no geographic justification. The tariff barriers of the Danubian region are without earthly logic. They create an unnatural politico-economic regionalism. In the nature of things they must go. Man may artificially erect regionalisms, but their test of endurance is environmental. The earth has time on its side, and conquers in the long run. Man is merely an interlude. The economic determinism to be recognized only in the broad historical sense is economic geography, the causal explanation of economic use. It is essentially economic areal contrast. The problem lies in the first instance of choosing and delimiting the area.

This volume started with a statement about the French Canadian *habitant*. I chose the Lower St. Lawrence as a subject for my doctor's thesis for rather sentimental reasons. One clear day in late September I was returning from England via the St. Lawrence route. The little shore settlements along the estuary intrigued me. On investigation, the region proved to be complete in definition; it was a simple area for study. Recently I made a reconnaissance of Belmont County, Ohio, as a thesis subject for a graduate student, and that region cannot be defined. The area of physical homogeneity, and the areas of tobacco raising, the dairy industry, and coal mining do not coincide with the county line, or with each other. Yet relief, agriculture and mining all enter the problem intimately interrelated. They are parts of the Belmont County complex. Moreover, the region should be treated historically, for these resource problems have changed their boundaries. Now if the problem the student is to undertake is not that of Belmont County, nor of any of the single economic factors in Belmont County, we have a distinct difficulty in naming the thesis. We might as well follow the lead of the musicians and call it "Opus No. 26" or "To a Wild Rose," then forget the title and make it a study of harmony, composition and counterpoint.

As an example of complexity let us take the Corn Belt. It happens to be industrial also, manufacturing agricultural machinery, food products, and a grand miscellany, but for fear of confusion we shall stick to tillage of the soil. In this east-west strip, there has evolved a definite culture from the days of Abraham Lincoln to the regional folk lore of "Babbitt," "Miss Lulu Bett" and the "Spoon River Anthology." It is a land of almost endless corn fields, bigger and better county fairs, and a great density of Rotary Clubs. It is the land of Hamlin Garland's "Son of the Middle Border." It is the Middle West, a land with a psychological consciousness.

To illustrate this, let me make a quotation. Willa Cather's book, "My Antonia," opens with: "Last summer I happened to be crossing the plains of Iowa in a season of great heat (corn weather).... While the train pushed through never-ending miles of ripe wheat, by country towns and bright-flowered pastures and oak groves wilting in the sun, we sat in the observation car, where the woodwork was hot to the touch and red dust lay deep over everything. The dust and heat, the burning wind reminded us of many things. We were talking about what it is like to spend one's childhood in little towns like these, buried in wheat and corn, under stimulating extremes of climate: burning summers when the world lies green and billowy beneath a brilliant sky, when one is fairly stifled in vegetation, in the color and smell of strong weeds and heavy harvests; blustery winters with little snow, when the whole country is stripped bare and gray as sheet-iron. We agreed that no one who had not grown up in a little prairie town could know anything about it. It was a kind of freemasonry, we said. . . ."

Further substantiation of this is given by J. Russell Smith:

"Corn Belt agriculture is not the hoe or garden type of agriculture, not saddle-supervision of a bunch of cowboys raising cattle, or a bunch of negroes raising cotton. Neither is it the foreman-bossing-a-gang-of-dagoes-weeding-onions type. It is the old, independent kingdom-of-my-own type, in which the farmer is nearly independent of outside labor. The farmer and his sons, with perhaps one hired man, do all the work, except at harvest time, when additional help is secured. The hired man is often a neighbor's son and the social equal of his employer. Few parts of the world, and no equally large part of the United States, can match the Corn Belt for social equality of the people."

The boundaries of the corn belt are all vague. Generally speaking, the western boundary is defined by 25 inches of annual rainfall; the northern boundary is the 70 degree mean summer isotherm; the eastern boundary lies where the limestone bedrock ceases and where the topography becomes hilly; and on the south the limits of glacial plains and somewhat hillier topography seem to have importance. But remember this, the corn belt is not where only corn grows, for one variety or another is grown in every state in the Union. It is where corn predominates, an area 900 miles wide to the east and west and 150 to 300 miles on the north and south. Its 150,000,000 acres, 8 percent of the arable land of the United States, include parts of Ohio, Indiana, Illinois, Iowa, Minnesota, Nebraska and a small part of Kansas. It has produced crops worth $325,000,-000,000, 25 percent of the country's crop value, and this on only 8 percent of the total farmed area. Its 850,000 farms are 13 percent of the farms of the country, yet they represent 35 percent of the total farm value. At boom prices, Iowa farms averaged a $50,000 value. Yields of corn, in so far as land was devoted to corn, were 3000 to 10,000 bushels to the square mile. Generally, if an area produced less than 3000 bushels to the square mile on the average it was considered outside of the corn belt. Each square mile produced on the average 5000 bushels of corn, 2500 bushels of oats, 1000 bushels of wheat, 150 tons of hay and fodder, with 140 acres left as pasture.

Corn is more valuable than wheat because it produces more bushels of grain to the acre, has industrial as well as food uses, and is in addition a fodder crop. Half of the corn is fed to swine, much of the rest to cattle. The industrial products are starch, sugar, syrup, cooking and salad oils, and breakfast food. This 8 percent of our tillable land produces 50 percent of the nation's corn and oats, 25 percent of the wheat and hay, feeds 20 percent of the cattle, 25 percent of the horses, 28 percent of the poultry, and 43 percent of the hogs. Texas is known for its cattle, and Kentucky for its horses, but the Corn Belt had 21,500,000 beasts of the farm in 1920.

If it is so grand a crop, why was corn not raised exclusively in this area? There is need for crop rotation, men must distribute their labor among many crops that harvest at different seasons, horses are needed for corn cultivation, and horses eat oats, while hay and fodder are necessary for roughage in cattle diet.

What are the physical circumstances which favor corn? Corn can be grown on steep hillsides by hoe labor but there one must have a mule with longer legs on one side than the other to do the plowing. Level land is best for working machinery, and rich soils are preferable. More critical conditions exist in climate. Corn is sensitive to frost and is planted later than other grains. Though some varieties mature in 80 or 90 days, the usual type requires a growing season of 120 to 150 days. Unlike most grains corn needs *continuously* high temperatures and warm nights. There should be 25 to 50 inches of rain a year of which at least 10 inches must fall in the growing season.

Miss Cather describes the climate as no statistics can: "July came on with that breathless brilliant heat which makes the plains of Kansas and Nebraska the best corn country in the world. It seemed as if we could hear the corn growing in the night; under the stars one caught a faint crackling in the dewy, heavy-odored cornfields where the feathered stalks stood so juicy and green."

And then: "Winter comes down savagely over a little town on the prairie. The wind that sweeps in from the open country strips away all the leafy screens that hide

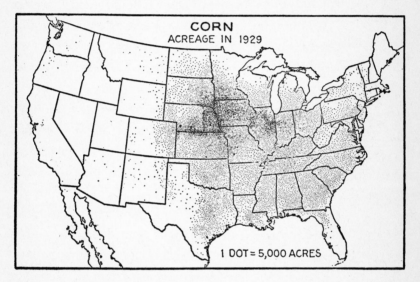

Fig. 21. The Corn Belt. The Department of Agriculture. Washington, D. C.

one yard from another in summer, and the houses seem to draw closer together.... Winter lies too long in country towns; hangs on until it is stale and shabby, old and sullen. On the farm the weather was the great fact and men's affairs went on underneath it, as the streams creep under the ice."

That is the corn belt, corn, corn, a farmhouse, wheat,

pasture, a feeding lot, a silo, corn, corn, windmills, square fields, and again corn endlessly. I once by chance flew above its length, and saw unbelievable orderliness, man's greatest agricultural achievement. The pleasant farm market towns made cool oases in the fields shimmering with summer heat. The plowing, planting, cultivating and harvesting of corn determines the rhythm of men's lives. As soon as the snow water has gone men plow. The rich prairie fields are turned up in glistening black furrows. I have seen two, three and four plows each drawn by five horses on great Iowa farms, with the huge barns standing in the midst of the fields like baronial castles. Today more and more men spend lonely hours riding back and forth across the huge fields on tractors. I wonder if they miss the companionship of the horse, but yet they must be able to dream of the beautiful crop to come.

Cultivation is under a hot June sun. Knee-high by the Fourth of July, corn cultivation ceases, and September finds it ready for harvest. Each state has its champion corn husker. The tallest stalk is fastened to the barn door, but the rest of the stalks are left to be "hogged down," to be eaten by the stock that disconsolately roams the muddy winter fields. A disordered and dreary scene. Elsewhere the corn is shocked. The barns are not large enough to store the bulky stalks so the farmer drives out to the frozen fields in winter to collect them as he has need. Perhaps winter wheat is planted before the stalks are collected, leaving eye-shaped empty spaces in the wheat field. Man may have planted the corn of his own volition, but once the crop is in the ground it controls his daily life and permeates his thoughts as surely as Wang Lung in "The Good Earth" was permeated by his land-consciousness.

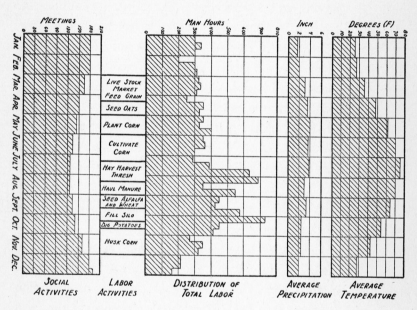

Fig. 22. A sociolograph of the corn belt, showing the round of the seasons.

This region has an agricultural prosperity such as the world knows nowhere else. The bounty of earth is beautiful. The same bounty means wealth. Retired corn farmers live in the market centers. Concrete road ribbons tie together towns, and there is an automobile for every farm. Thus the county church and the neighbor-

hood social have given place to the town church, the
movie theater and centralized social and political meet-
ings. The average town is a crossroads affair with two
main streets. A bank building, several churches, and
perhaps a county building, tower above the two-storied
edifices of the merchants. One street is shadier and has
the better houses, mostly of the cottage type with kitchen
gardens. Near the edge are the schools, and near the railroad station is a towering grain elevator, with some load-
ing pens for shipping livestock. Socially the town is
equipped with lodges and ladies' auxiliaries, poetry and
culture clubs. The American Legion runs a band and a
Protect-Our-Children campaign. The economic interests
are commercial banking, law, and medicine, and there
are a few retired farmers. Nor is the life entirely bucolic.
The well-to-do go to Chicago, Omaha, St. Louis or
New York for the theater and to wear their party
clothes. The larger towns support more cultural organ-
izations to the square mile than does any city, for they
feel their provincialism and work against it. I have in
mind so progressive a city as Freeport, Illinois.

Are these statistics enough to prove that the Corn
Belt is an economic complex with a distinct individuality? If not, geographers are ready to marshal more
numerical facts. They love them. Yet out of this land
of hot nights and silos has come a distinct cultural
contribution to our civilization, a contribution that began with Lincoln. In spite of egocentric life in New
York, Boston, San Francisco and Los Angeles, the Belt

is the heart of American democracy. Here is that generous freemasonry of which Miss Cather and Mr. Smith write. Here is a modern economic locality, without boundaries, yet with a definite human character. It is one of the modern, man-made complexities. It is a definite form of economy and it has a psychological response. Had we selected for study the vineyard lands of the Garonne valley in France, the wheat lands of Russia's Ukraine or the rice lands of the Mekong delta the story would have been the same.

Having the same definite character, the same lack of boundaries and yet as distinct a psychology are the modern industrial areas. Consider the central England manufacturing region, the area from Manchester to Birmingham, including man's disgrace, that smaller area known as the Black Country.

This Midland industrial section lies south of the Pennine hills and includes such centers as Manchester, Stoke, Birmingham, Sheffield, Leicester and Nottingham. Here are most of England's heavy industries such as steel and machinery manufacture, here are the textile mills, the shoe factories and the ceramic kilns. Manchester was a Roman town, for the "chester" indicates a camp. In the Middle Ages the town was devoted to woolen weaving because of water power from the Pennine hills and water for washing the wool. Today Manchester and its satellites form the greatest cotton cloth region in the world. Oldham makes medium-size threads, while Bolton and Preston have pride in larger threads. Blackburn and Burnely weave. Dye works are found at Widnes and St. Helen's. The whole land hums with spinning, or clatters with weaving. Forty-five million spindles, six hundred thousand looms, and five million people whose lives hang by a cotton thread, in colossal monotony. Two thousand and three hundred people to the square mile; two million, four hundred thousand persons within twelve miles of the stock exchange of Manchester. There is lint in the air, and lint is in the lungs.

West Riding sounds like a fox hunt. It lies in Yorkshire which sounds like a pudding. Seventy-eight million tons of coal were mined from this region in 1929. Sheffield makes excellent steel from imported Swedish ores. Sheffield makes every steel product from razor blades to armor plate. Its 512,000 inhabitants live in a setting of dirty hills and black smokestacks.

In Staffordshire are the potteries, and a man-made environment effaces the native landscape completely. Arnold Bennett was an authority on the "Five Towns." Really six, they are now organized as Stoke-on-Trent. In a region rich in clay and coal, there are eight miles of potteries. The landscape is one of chimneys, furnaces, warehouses and drying-houses. Here is made the famous Staffordshire ware, and in the local squares stand begrimed statues of Wedgwood and Minton. The land is busy with industry, and the nearby railway center of Crewe is visited by 600 trains daily. Yet just beyond is the graceful Lichfield Cathedral, and the peaceful streams where Izaak Walton once fished.

Bennett described the separate individuality of the factory towns in "The Old Wives' Tale":

"The fact is, that while in the county they (the sisters) were also in the district; and no person who lives in the district, even if he should be old and have nothing to do but reflect upon things in general, ever thinks about the county (the country side). So far as the county goes, the district might almost as well be in the middle of the Sahara. . . . It lies on the face of the county like an insignificant stain, like a dark Pleiades in a green and empty sky . . . the architecture of the Five Towns is an architecture of ovens and chimneys . . . its atmosphere is as black as its mud . . . it burns and smokes all night, so that Longshaw has been compared to hell . . . it lives crammed together in slippery streets where the housewife must change white window curtains at least once of a fortnight. All the everyday crockery used in the kingdom is made in the Five Towns—all and much besides."

Birmingham has nearby the epitome of manufacturing in an area just north of the city known as the Black Country.

Visit the region with Priestley, who wrote:

"There was the Black Country unrolled before you like a smouldering carpet. You looked into an immense hollow of smoke and blurred buildings and factory chimneys. There seemed to be no end to it. In the vague middle, dominating everything, was an enormous round white tower, which I afterwards learned was a new gasometer. It looked bigger than anything else in sight, and as nothing had dimension that could be measured, it was any size you liked to imagine it. You could think of it, without unduly straining your fancy, as the temple of some horrible new religion. The only sounds that arrived from this misty immensity below came from the tangle of railway lines that gleamed in the foreground of the scene, and these noises were so clear that they might have been picked out and then amplified. There was the scream of a locomotive; there was the clanking of the bumped wagons; there was the long pu-u-ushing of a train gathering speed. I never remember hearing these railway sounds so clearly. Nothing else came from the enormous hollow. You could easily believe that there were no people down there, that a goods locomotive was probably the most playful inhabitant of the region. I was glad that I did not know the names of the towns down there in the smoke; I felt that I was not looking at this place and that, but at the metallic Midlands themselves, at a relief map of a heavy industry, at another and greater exhibition of the 'fifties. No doubt at all that the region had a somber beauty of its own. I thought so then, and I thought so later, when I had seen far more of its iron face lit with hell fire. But it was a beauty you could appreciate chiefly because you were not condemned to live there. If I could do what I liked with the whole country, I would keep a good tract of this region as it is now, to be stared and wondered at; but I would find it difficult to ask any but a few curators to live in it."

Have I contrasted the environment of the manufacturing Midlands of England with that of the corn-producing midlands of America sufficiently to indicate that there must be a differing psychology? Some one else will have to characterize the mind of the industrial proletariat—I do not know enough about it. But lives devoted to middle-size threads, to the manufacture of a single type of brick, the assembly-line mind *must* have a quality different from the mind of our corn growers.

Every great industrial land has its Black Country. I was raised on the outskirts of South Chicago and saw its hellishness and its vulgarity extend over the sandy plains as far as Gary, Indiana. I do not know of an area where the embellishments were so lacking. Cheap rooming houses, dirty saloons, miserable picture houses, ice cream spas, pulp magazines, nothing else. I once visited Youngstown, Ohio, and traversed a valley mutilated by iron, steel and cinders. In town I could hardly see for smoke. At the Chamber of Commerce they regretted that I had come when they were working at only sixteen percent of capacity! Thank God, I was spared a hundred percent grime.

So much for our modern complexes. So much for the smudges which we have created. So much for the unsanitary regions we call slums which Watt, Stevenson and Fulton made possible by their inventions. In these areas tons of soot are breathed in by the unfortunate inhabitants. Culturally, their contributions to Man must be more largely material than spiritual, unless evolving from them comes the humanity of socialism.

Chapter Thirteen

THE GEOGRAPHY OF

NATIONAL COMPETITION

WARS ARISE FROM CONDITIONS WHICH HAVE EXISTED
for decades and even centuries. The events which led
to the World War did not suddenly appear in 1914.
They had fundamentally to do with the adjustments
of increasing populations, but dividing Europe into
armed camps was an expression of provincialism. This
provincialism was of a new and more complex sort
than that which we have described, and was epitomized
by the purely political term, nationalism. Nations are
as old as history. Nationalism is a psychology quite
modern, an intensification of regional ambition, eco-

nomic aims and pride of homeland encouraged by the
governments to strengthen the nation as it competes
for its place in the sun.

Such a spirit is at times as artificial as cheering under
a cheerleader in a stadium. And its exaggeration of the
local virtues is frequently humorous. When I first came
to Ohio I was seriously given to understand that people
from Indiana were inferior. Three-fourths of Ohio is
quite like Indiana and the remainder definitely like
West Virginia. But I remind my students that in at
least one regard the state does lead all others. Ohio is
foremost in manufacturing sewer pipe, and Columbus
is the false-tooth center of the world. I can remember
that in grade school I was convinced any American
could whip six Mexicans, and that we had the biggest
and best of everything. This is no funnier than the
Nordic claims of today. I reproduce a map made in
Germany while Hitler was still a corporal. We laugh
at it because we know that Greek and Roman culture
came directly to America, perhaps through Baltimore.
Yet these national prides must be taken seriously. They
are very important.

Out of the Middle Ages arose the artificial provincialisms of nations. England, defined as it was by water
and Scotch, was early in developing a national sense.
This was emphasized as Henry VII added to his
kingly authority. In the reign of Elizabeth the increasing national consciousness was exemplified by the pop-
ularity of the writings of Richard Hakluyt, exploits of

sea heroes. Though Hakluyt was a man of the cloth, these are rather bloody. Strange that pride is often a measure of the blood of enemies that has been spilled. Only a little earlier in this same period Spain was pass-

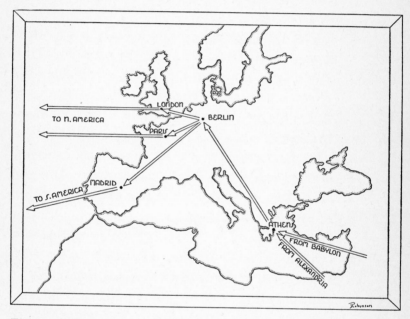

Fig. 23. A German concept of how the Americas received their cultures.

ing through her Renaissance, evolving a national pride after the defeat of the Moors and the exploration and exploitation of the Americas. These feats gave the Spaniards a glory in their possession of their own territory, and in the accumulation of other people's bullion. Such glory justified an arrogance which led to the slaughter

of the Caribs, Aztecs and Incas. Iberia shared with
England definite boundaries for her growing provincialism. Nationalism is a psychic form of provincialism
which brooks no transitions, no half-hearted support.
It must have complete allegiance. One is either a Greek
or a barbarian, and physical boundaries are great aids
in drawing a distinction which otherwise might be
difficult. The Alsace-Lorraine region is a transition between Germany and France, and it is only with difficulty that first one country and then the other forces
its own national culture upon those people.

France well illustrates my view of the complexity of
the new national provincialism. France has many definite provinces, each contrasted with its neighbor. These
contrasts make it a country where regional geography
can be illustrated with exactness and finesse. The various
regions were held by feudal lords who were, except for
the title, provincial kings, and the king of France was
little more than chairman of a board of dukes until
Richelieu, under Louis XIII, conceived a united France,
and theorized about natural frontiers. The growing
national consciousness became a passion with Louis
XIV. He gloried in unifying the nation, in consolidat-
ing the marginal feudal holdings to—well, mark off
the Greeks from the barbarians. Authority became so
centered that it was personified by Louis. He was the
Sun King; he was the State, divine right in person. It
was necessary to give geographical limitations to such
divinity, and Richelieu had done that. The Pyrenees,

the Alps and, of course, the sea were obvious limits. And then the idea of the Rhine as a boundary took hold of the French mind.

During this period, kingly authority, especially in England, gained over the dukes and feudal lords because it was supported by the merchant middle class. Commerce, not being agricultural or land holding and breaking down isolation, was essentially anti-feudal. The kings were receiving monies from the coffers of the merchants with which to weaken the already decentralized feudal power. Also, this was a period of overseas expansion. Merchants were conflicting and fighting with men of other countries. They needed protection, needed navies, and turned to the kings they supported for that aid. They must put off the seas the dastardly foreigners who infringed upon their profits. The rivalry between France and England was as old as the Hundred Years' War when the Flanders wool trade, Gascony wine trade, and profits from fisheries brought the two countries to strife. The struggle for the Spanish Main was a competition which national religious attitudes intensified.

We cannot detail the growth of all the nations. Every country coming under a centralized authority, creating definite boundaries, in this modern period had one or all of these three attributes: historical tradition, natural geographical unity, or fanatical leadership. After 1815 we find a new country, Belgium. Metternich,

the consistent Austrian reactionary, was opposing anything and everything in the new order, so he opposed
the creation of Belgium. It was and is a country without natural boundaries. Geographically, it does not
make sense; it was without historical tradition as
bounded, for one-third of Flanders is in France; and it
had no leaders, no common language and no common
religion. No wonder Metternich opposed it. Belgium
is an example to prove that nationalism is not always
geographic in origin, and that your present environmentalist has not gone completely mad.

To prove that the geographic factor *does* play a part,
remember the unification of Italy. So logical is the
coincidence there of soil and state that it is hard to
understand how Italy could have been so disjointed as
it was in 1815. It is a perfect physiographic province,
and it had the best of historical tradition. It came to
have leaders: Mazzini, Cavour and Garibaldi. National
unity was for a period a latent potentiality. When they
were given leadership, almost overnight twenty-two
million inhabitants found their political hearts beating
with a single pulse.

Prussia was a scattered group of feudal possessions.
Frederick the Great bemoaned its lack of natural
boundaries. Lying as it did upon an extensive plain,
it was written that Prussia must extend herself to the
plain's natural frontier or be submerged. Remember,
Latium had the same problem. Prussia had great lead-

ership and, like the Romans, a well-trained army. But there are not many decisive boundaries to the Prussian plain. Bismarck was never certain what the limits of Prussian expansion should be; nor is Hitler. Considering Hitler's recent acquisitions, it must be remembered that empires which take in diverse and separated provinces are geographically weak; the writer's personal opinion is that natural provinces eventually reassert themselves. The Germans have used *Kultur* to further their nationalism: the composers of music did much; historians, like Hegel, have done their part; and the now disgraced Heine wrote his poetry in that spirit. Do not remind me that I have wandered from environmentalism; I am now concerned with man-conceived expressions of regionalism.

Eventually, we came to have political entities known as nations. Whatever their character, they were bound to a special bit of soil upon this over-crowded world. Europe was, in terms of the times, too well-populated, so the new nations eyed each other with green hate. This hate was nationalism and a measure of strength. Since industrial developments were demanding raw materials and markets, a second period of expansion was begun, capitalistic imperialism. The details are interesting, pure history. Let us be factual and statistical.

In 1771 there were perhaps 145,000,000 people in Europe. By 1871 this figure had reached 293,000,000. Today, Europe contains possibly 500,000,000 persons.

The increase in mouths to be fed had by 1871 created serious problems. The countries with the greater problems are indicated by the following tables: *

Belgium	425 *persons to the square mile*
Holland	285
United Kingdom	261
Italy	242
German Empire	205
France	182
Austria	176
Switzerland	173
Hungary	125
Poland	123

It would seem that Belgium and Holland had the greatest problems, but both are known for their great food production. The United Kingdom concentrated most of its population in England, and England produced little food. Here then was a definite problem. Italy solved a similar problem by a low standard of living. The German Empire turned to manufacturing as a means of livelihood. France produces more food more easily than Germany. England and Germany went into an almost desperate competition for markets.

Europe cleared her forests in order to have more farm lands. Swamps were drained. Scientific agriculture in-

* The several tables are from Clive Day's "History of Commerce."

creased farm production per acre. How the acreage under crops increased is shown by these figures:

In 1820 there were 364,000,000 acres under crops
1840   427,000,000
1860   471,000,000
1880   546,000,000

The four densely populated countries that had coal built more factories. In 1870 their production was:

United Kingdom   *120,700,000 tons a year*
German Empire   *43,100,000*
France   *15,100,000*
Belgium   *13,700,000*

At this time the United States was producing a tonnage about equal to that of Germany.

The importance of this is that it shows the extent to which England was becoming industrial. Industry needs markets, and England was the first to seize the markets. But after 1870 both Germany and the United States increased their output from factories. The output of the United States was largely absorbed by home markets, but the goods which Germany manufactured largely went into foreign trade, and Germany became a serious competitor of England.

Let us compare the trade of England during three periods:

	Imports	*Exports*
1860-64	$ 965,000,000	$ 690,000,000
1885-94	1,590,000,000	1,130,000,000
1910-13	3,055,000,000	2,370,000,000

In 1885 England had about one-fourth of the trade of the world. In 1912 England had one-sixth of the trade. Not only was England's commerce increasing by leaps and bounds, but other countries were increasing at an even more rapid rate. England kept the lead because it was best developed industrially, because it was well situated, and because commerce was king in England. Trade was the backbone of English economy and it was treated with reverence and wisdom. The imports were largely foodstuffs, for England had become so industrial and so over-populated that there was never food enough in the country at any one time to feed the people for more than a month. Raw materials for the textile industries, and later iron ore, were also large imports.

You will note in the above table that the imports exceed the exports. They did also in ancient Rome. Centers of empire offer political services for food. But in these modern times, the difference between the value of imports and exports is paid for largely with the dividends from capital invested abroad. Do not forget that modern imperialism is capitalistic imperialism. All this commerce called for a huge merchant fleet and a protecting navy. England was perforce mistress of the seas. In 1914 the British owned almost half of the world's sea tonnage. So great were her ship-building yards that she manufactured ships for other nations, and in the twenty years previous to the World

War built two-thirds of all the ships constructed in the world.

At the opening of the twentieth century English commerce developed new trends. The quantity of commerce was not declining, but the quality was cheaper. The profit of a factory depends upon the labor put into the making of the product. There was less profit in these cheaper manufactures. England was losing rank among the trading nations in both quantity and quality, but her population was still growing. England was worried. Germany realized this and increased her army.

In 1850 German industrial output was of no great importance, but it had increased ten times by 1900. The first great step in the increase of German industry came with the formation of the Zollverein. This was a customs union, begun in 1828, which allowed free transit of goods between the various German states. In the period 1870-1913 the population of Germany increased sixty-three percent. The 67,000,000 people could not be fed at home. Many immigrated to the United States. Greater numbers were fed through the sale of German manufactures. In this period German foreign trade increased 250 percent, four times as fast as the population.

The chief bases of German industry were coal and iron, and she had numerous and extensive coal fields. In the newly-acquired Lorraine (taken by the Franco-Prussian War) were huge quantities of low-grade iron ore. German invention made possible the conversion of this ore, and the German steel industry became a serious competitor of the British. Moreover, Germany offered the best technical education for workers, and her universities were superior to all in their scientific laboratories. German salesmen covered the world, talking fluently the languages of the people to whom they sold.

The reasons which lay back of the failure of the French to take part in this new industrial competition are much the same as those which had kept her from playing her expected role in the period of expansion. Only quite recently had the French realized the importance of imperialism, and French population increases were not as great as in the other countries, so industry was less essential. The French spirit seemed to make the people more content to tend their vineyards and cabbage patches, which they did with great skill. Moreover, France has more fertile soil than either of the countries we have just discussed; she did not lack food. When the French did take to manufactures it frequently was to produce artistic luxuries, and the other countries did not compete with French artistry.

Two reasons why France had not developed the "heavy" industries were the modest deposits of coal, and the major lack of iron ore. Lorraine contained great iron ore deposits but these were taken by Germany as spoils of the Franco-Prussian war, yet the loss of the iron ore affected the French far less than the sentimental loss of Alsace and Lorraine. In Paris, where each province is represented by a statue, the figures for the two lost provinces were draped in black. France watched for an opportunity to reclaim Alsace and Lorraine, but each year saw Germany becoming stronger.

This does not complete the picture of the nations with teeth bared, but enough has been said to show how a situation was created from which no mere diplomat could hope to extricate his country. If economically the countries had been able to make adjustments, there remained the psychology of race hatreds based upon provincialisms and encouraged by rampant nationalisms. Diplomats attempted to hold up the house of cards by lies and alliances, a paper-support of peace called the Balance of Power. The balance of power set up by the Congress of Vienna was upset by the Franco-Prussian War, and Prussia, grown into the German Empire, had actually taken provinces from France. More than this, her industries were taking markets from Britain. Germany was the nightmare of Europe. At the Congress of Berlin, Germany had begun making treaties to increase her power, supporting Italy against France, and Austria against Russia. To withstand the threatening hordes of the east an alliance of Germany, Austria-Hungary and Italy was formed. Austria joined Germany in the Triple Alliance because of their mutual fear of Russia. Italy joined because she was afraid of a French invasion. Geographically, these three countries formed a north-south zone from the Baltic to the Mediterranean, which gave Germany a southern sea coast.

There was a counter-force to the Triple Alliance created for the balance of power, the Triple Entente. The Kaiser had said that no important political move, in Europe or over-seas, could be made without taking Germany into account. England, as an island power, was isolated from continental politics. Her interests were as mediator, that is, she hoped to maintain the balance of power. Also, she was engaged, and too-successfully engaged, in empire building to take an active part in European affairs. She was, however, interested in the neutrality of Belgium, for through Belgium, England *might* be invaded. However, Germany was interfering with English imperialistic markets, upsetting the balance of power. During the Boer War, England's high-handed policy isolated her from her neighbors, so she could not now curb Germany alone. A friendship developed between England and France, and England made friends with Russia, partly through fear. England, France and Russia, the Triple Entente, were thus aligned against Germany, Austria and Italy, the Triple Alliance.

The basic causes of war lay in national competition and national dislike, but there were three tinder boxes from which the conflagration might start. Each had its geographical aspect. The first was the Balkan Question, the question of seizing portions of the disorganized Balkans. In 1912-1913 there had been local wars in that area. The first was to throw out the Turk, and the second to squabble over the spoils of victory. Greece had boundaries established by tradition. There was obvious geographical sense to the boundaries of Rumania and Bulgaria. But the area which is today Yugoslavia was not physically unified, it lacked a main street. Greece had had sea-ways. The Balkan interior had none. Austria-Hungary began absorbing the northern provinces, endangering the aforesaid balance of power.

There was yet another region whose stability was not established, and in which lay the possibility of upsetting Europe. This was the Austrian-Hungarian Empire itself. It was an alliance and empire which had certain economic justification, but within which smoldered suppressed provincialisms and racial hatreds.

Vienna, the capital of Austria, had been a bulwark against the Turks in 1683. It had grown into a country, expanding along the trade routes to the west. Thus the Central Alps became Austrian. It expanded beyond the Alps via the Brenner Pass, until it controlled northern Italy. Later, the line was thrown back but Austria continued to hold one province on the south side of the Brenner Pass, the South Tyrol. It also held an area about the end of the Adriatic, with Trieste as the sole Austrian outlet on the sea.

Next door, and to the east of Austria, lay Hungary. Hungary, too, had fought the Turks and had thrown them back beyond the southern Carpathian Mountains. Hungary produced livestock and wheat and little else. It was not economically self-sufficient. Therefore, it was with a certain logic that Hungary was joined to Austria which was more industrial, had a variety of agricultural products, and was a dairy country. Together, they included all of the central European depression surrounded by mountains. They were both a physical and economic unit. One statesman paraphrasing Voltaire said, "If Austria-Hungary did not exist some one would have invented it."

But the Austrians were Germans and the Hungarians were Magyars, different peoples speaking a different language. In addition there were included in the empire Czechs (Bohemians), Germans in Bohemia, Slovaks, Ruthenians, Rumanians, Tiroleans, Bavarians, and Yugoslavs. These people were not nationalized, but they continued to retain their individualism due to strong physical provincialisms. Austria-Hungary was more an economic than a political unit.

The third tinder box was more commercial than territorial. Berlin, or more particularly the Kaiser, became interested in a relatively undeveloped field of expansion, the rich Mesopotamian valley. This valley was isolated by desert and its harborless coast, and had been overlooked in the scramble for imperialistic territory. The Kaiser saw opportunities there, but between Germany and Mesopotamia lay Austria and Turkey. Austria was German in sympathy and race, and its politics were more or less dictated from Berlin. Turkey was a neglected ally and easily flattered. The Kaiser made overtures with compliments to Turkey. A railway was to be built from Berlin to Bagdad in Mesopotamia, with a ferry over the Bosporus. This railway was planned in 1903 and was to be on German or Turkish territory. German manufacturers were delighted with the prospect of new markets. England became greatly concerned. Here was a new short route to India, and it threatened the English sea route. But Germany went ahead with her plans.

This does not complete the story. Every overseas colony complicated the matter. With no regard for humanity or justice, the powers scrambled to be first in imperialistic perfidy, and seize upon lands with less progressive culture. The Great African Hunt began. Spheres of influence in the east were created without apology, much less any theoretical justification. The Monroe Doctrine must have been a blow to the European nations.

National competition was basic in causing the first World War. Nationalism and racial hatred were expressions of this competition. The murder of an archduke had as little significance as the stealing of Helen in the Trojan War.

Chapter Fourteen

THE GEOGRAPHY OF EUROPE

IS ONE OF CONFLICT

WHATEVER THE CAUSES, HOWEVER MUCH THEY WERE from geographic realism, from blunders of deceptive diplomats, or from the age-old urge of men to fight, we had a war in 1914. Essentially it was based upon the geographic principle that the state is derived ultimately from the ownership of a bit of soil. Proudly we called it the World War; now it has become the *first* World War. It devastated soil and man and the works of man. I suppose we permit such inane catastrophes because abstract virtues like peace and love are difficult to comprehend, whereas a stone-ax is a concrete, comprehensible thing, a man's weapon. Besides, war is a habit with us. Visiting Martians, after their recent trip here, are said to have reported to their luncheon club brethren in Rotary that war was our dominant cultural characteristic.

The character of the land for which men fight, and on which they fight, is of supreme importance. Remember how a few Greeks stood at narrow Thermopylae until the Persians were able to outflank them by a secret pass. And there is the classic example of Napoleon's defeat on the Russian plain because it was too vast and too cold. But we need not go back beyond the World War.

The objective of the westward German drive was Paris. Paris lies in a geologic basin. It is as if saucers were placed within each other, each successive saucer being smaller. Paris is in the center of such a basin and is surrounded by concentric ridges representing the edges of the upturned rocks. As in the diagram map, each ridge is gently sloped inward, but on the east it has a steep slope hindering the German advance. At the bottom of these steep slopes there is usually a river with marshy banks. The French were able to place artillery on the crests of these ridges which forced the Germans to cross an exposed plain, ford a river, and climb a cliff before capturing the French position.*

---

* Any writer on the geography of the World War must, as do I, owe gratitude to D. W. Johnson who wrote "Topography and Strategy in the War."

There were a number of these ridges to form natural defenses for Paris. Nearest Paris were the two Champagne ridges. A third was known as the Argonne, and beyond lay Verdun. There the most terrific battle of the war was fought. Last of all came the Metz ridge. Through all these were river passes, and gateways; each held a commercial city, and in each there were a series of fortresses. South of the Paris basin, the French had a natural defense barrier in the Vosges Mountains, wooded and with considerable height. They also sloped gently to the west, presenting a steep face to Germany.

There were a number of natural passageways from Germany into France. The most southern was the open area between the east-west Jura Mountains on the French border and the north-south Vosges Mountains. This was so low that a canal had been dug through it to connect the Rhône River with the Rhine, guarded by the city of Belfort and numerous fortifications. It was so narrow as to be easily defended, so the Germans failed to take it in the Franco-Prussian War, and did not even attempt to do so in the World War.

The second opening was the Metz gateway, north of the Vosges. This was the Alsace-Lorraine plain, held at the outset of the war by the Germans. It seemed the logical approach for the Germans, but it must be remembered that they planned to dash into France, overcome that country in quick order, and then turn their attention to the Russians. After Metz, the Germans

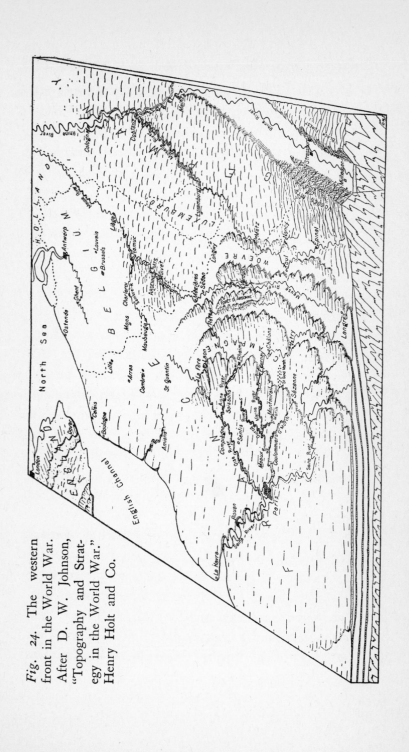

Fig. 24. The western front in the World War. After D. W. Johnson, "Topography and Strategy in the World War." Henry Holt and Co.

would still have to conquer the several ridges that defended Paris, which promised to be a slow process.

North of the plain was an upland known as the Ardennes, broken by two river gorges, the Moselle and the Meuse. These rivers led to the Rhine and were natural highways, but they lay below a plateau. As passageways they were dangerous, and after the plateau was won, there still remained the ridges around Paris.

The only remaining way into France was over the Belgian plain, so the Germans quickly destroyed the frontier fortifications and advanced. The plain was monotonous, low ridges gave only slight opportunities for defense, and railways and roads were numerous and excellent, which permitted the great German military machine to quickly invade France and flank the ridges which defended the other approaches to Paris.

With unbelievable rapidity they poured through Belgium. The strong fortress of Liege, in eastern Belgium, withstood the huge siege guns for only three days, and within two weeks the German columns marched in goosestep through Brussels. The Belgians fought fiercely, but the Germans crushed them and drove the remnants of the army on to French soil. Before the French had fully awakened to their plight, German scouting forces were within fifteen miles of Paris.

Two things happened. First, it became necessary to take part of the German forces from France to hold back the Russians (anyway, it seemed Paris was about to fall). Second, the French, retreating and retreating, were gathering greater numbers. At the Marne River, the French under General Joffre made a stand and turned back the onrushing enemy. In the meantime, English, Belgian, and more French soldiers stopped the northern German advance, before the channel ports communicating with England were taken. Then the Germans dug in. They built miles and miles of trenches, dugouts, and half-buried fortresses guarded by barbed wire entanglements. Trench warfare had begun.

The battle of the Marne turned the tide of the German advance. The French and English, taking fullest advantage of physical features, gradually forced the Germans back to the gorge of the Aisne River, which gave the Germans such strength that the allies were unable to dislodge them.

The Germans occupying Lorraine now attempted to break through a pass in the ridges that defended Paris, which was the battle of Nancy. For a fortnight the Germans stormed the Nancy ridge, and forty thousand of them died at the base of the cliff.

The greatest battle was the attack on the Verdun-Toul ridge. The Germans were forced to cross an open plain which lay to the east of the line of hills. The slaughter was terrible, but in one place the Germans gained a foothold. Never before had such an accumulation of troops and munitions been achieved. For weeks the forts on the crest of the hill above Verdun received a continuous rain of steel and high explosives. Trenches were taken and retaken, again and again.

The French slogan was, "They shall not pass," and they did not pass, but both sides paid heavily.

Russia had huge forces, and it looked as if the Russian mass might roll on into Germany, forcing aside the German defense with its very weight. Prussia, Russia and Austria had divided Poland between them. Poland was more or less without natural barriers and Russia advanced into German territory without being hindered by physical features. Let us look at the geography of the area.

The battle ground was in what was later to be Poland. This area had four provinces. The southernmost was the Carpathian Zone. The Carpathian Mountains of the north were forested and wild, with little population, and a number of low, gorge-like passes easily defended from above, all many miles apart. The Russians took command of them but did not dare to use them to descend upon the Hungarian plain.

The second province was the plateau and hill region north of the mountains known as Podolia. Beyond that lay the wet, low, flat plain of the Vistula. Adjacent to the Baltic, the last province, was a ridge country of confusing hills and swamps.

The obvious passage to Germany was by the plain. But the Russians did not dare force a passage unless the hills were cleared of Germans, and Podolia cleared of the Austrians; they did not want the enemy on their flanks. In the hills they met defeat. The Germans, under von Hindenberg, won the battle of Tannenberg

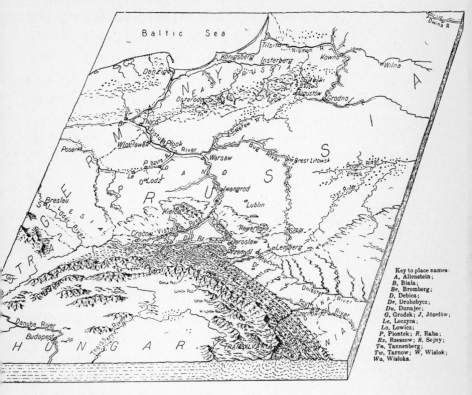

Fig. 25. The eastern front in the World War. After D. W. Johnson, "Topography and Strategy in the World War." Henry Holt and Co.

and some 80,000 Russians were trapped and slaughtered. To make a long story short, the Germans then advanced over the muddy Polish plain. The Russians used the north-flowing rivers and the morasses as defense lines, but each in turn was taken.

The year 1915 was disastrous for the Russians: the

Germans held the Baltic Sea; the English closed the Dardanelles; and the one port on the Arctic Ocean usually ice-free now froze. Russia was not industrial and depended largely upon the outside world for munitions and machines of war. War materials now could come only from Japan by the long, single-tracked, poorly-built Trans-Siberian Railroad, and Germany bribed Russian officials to delay shipments. The Russian Army without shells offered a resistance only by numbers; the slaughter was pitiful. Germany soon held Russian territory, the Russian threat was gone; and Germany could transfer troops to other borders. Bulgaria, heartened by the successes of the Central Powers, joined them in the fight.

Italy, pledged to the Triple Alliance, turned against the Central Powers. She had long felt hatred for Austria because the Italians once held the Po Valley, and because Italy wished to possess the head of the Adriatic. The Allies made secret promises of territory to Italy so that she declared war on Austria-Hungary in May, 1915, hoping to push Austria back over the crest of the Alps. The Italian soldiers clamored for war, shouting *"Italia Irredenta"* (Italy Unredeemed) and *"Avante Savoie"* (Forward Savoy).

So began a war in a most strange land. The Italian Alps are high with isolated peaks and glaciers, so the soldiers became mountaineers and alpinists, and wore white so that they could not be seen against the snow. Cannon were dragged to almost inaccessible peaks.

Food, munitions, and men were transported on wires high into the mountains. Tunnels were built through mountains to make openings for cannon. Other tunnels permitted the blowing up of forts. Great piles of stones were dropped on attackers. Trenches were often in snow and ice, and gun fire started avalanches. Small groups of men at advantageous points controlled whole valleys. The Italian advance was by trickery and cunning rather than force, but the Austrians made a mass attack, secretly bringing great numbers of troops into the mountains. The Italians were surprised and fell back, though the Austrians lacked numbers with which to follow up their success.

Further east, the Austrians possessed the plain and the Carso Plateau, a limestone upland pitted with sink holes, and undermined with caves and passages. The sink holes and caves afforded what seemed an almost impregnable defense position. The Italians swept easily as far as the plateau but then progress was slow. Men tunneled and counter-tunneled to blow up positions. No maneuvers such as those on the Polish plain were possible. Each mile was fought for desperately, and the advance was largely underground.

In the meantime, war in the Balkans was confused because of the character of the land. Serbia was early attacked by Austria-Hungary. The small and ill-equipped Serbian army was aided by the rough country and fought stubbornly. In October, 1915, Germans, Austrians, and Bulgars threatened Serbia. Greece, aided by an allied force, met the Bulgars, but then refused support to the Serbs, who were badly exposed to the enemy and quite without artillery. Defeating the Serbs was merely a matter of time, especially when the Bulgarians entered the attack; Slavs against Slavs. The allies supported Serbia from Salonika on the Aegean coast, a port well defended by mountains, with access to a valley leading into the heart of the Balkans.

Rumania was on the side of the allies, though practically isolated. Hungary to the north and Bulgaria to the south were hostile. The water route was closed by Turkey, and the only contact with the allies was through Russia. When Rumania entered the war in 1916, Russia was of no help.

That Rumania should turn against the Central Powers created a difficulty for Turkey, for Turkey obtained munitions from Germany, and Rumania threatened to cut the rail route. Moreover, Rumania was particularly valuable to the Central Powers because of her wheat and oil production. Germany turned her attention to the problem and in a short time her armies had overrun the Rumanian plain. An 800-mile battle front was thus shortened in a few days to 300 miles, freeing more men for the fight on the western front.

Of course, men fought in the air, in tunnels and in submarines. But essentially they fought as they have always, and will always, for a bit of land. They fought for provinces and were not satisfied until they held the strategic ridge at the far sides of the province. The character of campaigns was controlled by the form of the terrain. Indeed, the causes of war as well as the alignment of the allies was geographic. Here was one of the oldest motifs in history—a sense of provincialism. The physical provincialisms tried again to become states. The wheat-producing Ukraine hoped to break from Russia. The Yugoslavs wished to limit Austrian power to the north side of the Karawanken Alps. Italy was demanding that the crest of the Tirolean Alps become a boundary. Bohemia, the chief and well-defined province of Czechoslovakia, was establishing independence. France insisted upon Louis XIII's conception of physical boundaries, the bank of the Rhine.

Geographic facts are largely concerned with man's adjustment to the varieties of earthly circumstance. Earlier in this volume there were examples of man's complete ignoring of nature's kindly suggestions. In no way does he more conspicuously ignore physical circumstances than in his marking of political boundaries. For example, one would think of the sea coast as a definite and exact boundary, but even there man cannot come to a decision. All countries agree that national boundaries should be extended out to sea for three miles, an hour's sail by wind. In our fine rum-running days we extended this to twelve miles, an hour's run for a power boat, and Great Britain followed suit. Italy claims 20 miles, but then Italy seems about to claim *all* of *Mare Nostrum*. One must admit that tidal flats make the seashore a fluctuating boundary; I have seen land at low tide extended three miles beyond high water. Islands are outer fortifications, but on the other hand islands are stepping stones for invaders. Typical are the Channel Islands, Guernsey, Jersey and Alderney. By geographic right they are French, but actually and politically they are English. More dramatic is the Italian possession of Cherso which so effectively guards the way to Yugoslavian Sušak, the alienated suburb of Fiume. Less important but equally threatening is Italy's possession of the Dalmatian island of Lagosta. Brief reading in political geographies will bring forth other examples.

Then there are mountains. Obvious boundaries, or are they? Van Valkenberg refers to cheval countries, countries riding astride, and gives us this map of Rumania and Bulgaria. During wars any defendable ridge is for a time a boundary; as witness the forested ridge of the Argonne. One of the weaknesses of mountains as barriers is that rivers may run athwart them. The Garonne River, for example, rises on the Spanish side of the chief crests of the Pyrenees. A small area, the Val d'Aran, tributary to France in its natural slope, is Spanish, but it is isolated from Spain by a high mountain wall and from France by a tariff barrier. Because main mountain crests, always strategically important, do not coincide with drainage lines, the upper course of the Inn river is Swiss, the middle is Austrian, and the lower course German. The upper portion, the

Engadine, is reached by the Swiss only through the arduous and difficult Albula Pass.

There is another difficulty in using mountains as boundaries. Alpine villages are less concerned with

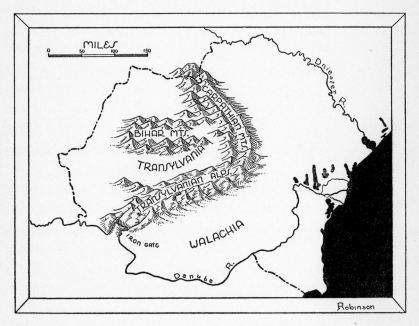

Fig. 26. A cheval country. Rumania as it was in 1929. After Van Valkenburg.

lands downstream than with high pastures. Economically they look upward to the alps which pasture their herds in summer. On the opposite side are similar villages which share the problems of protecting, using, and properly dividing the grasslands. The high communities have a common culture and economic interest, even though their political affiliations may be different. Though Paris and Madrid called upon communities in the Pyrenees for allegiance, there existed among the Spanish and French mountaineers a confederation, an extra-political confederation, which lasted for three hundred years, and there are still remnants today. These altitudinal cultures can be called straddle cultures. That Switzerland extends over the Alps and down the Italian side to a spot midway on the slope would classify her as a straddle culture, in part at least.

The most important example of this is the Tirol. Tirolean culture is a high-level herding and wood-cutting economy. Properly speaking, it does not extend down into the mixed farming and industrial areas of the Austrian valley of the Inn. On the Italian side it ceases where one meets the vine culture, a culture divided in two by Italian insistence upon the alpine crest as a strategic and defensive boundary. The Italians do not want the Austrians holding an upper slope in a drainage area tributary to their plains. Needless to say, the German-speaking South Tiroleans, with a fine historical tradition which connects them to the North Tiroleans, are most unhappy under Italian control. Recently it was reported they had been expelled entirely.

Rivers as boundaries are of varying value. A geologically young river sunken in a gorge is a good boundary. The Grand Canyon could well serve as a boundary. But broad rivers are frequently used as national limits;

the Danube for 100 miles served Czechoslovakia as a border. Between Rumania and Bulgaria the Danube is bordered by swamps and difficult to cross because of floating islands so it is a satisfactory barrier. But mature or old rivers (see any physiography or physical geography for the proper reading of these terms) are not the best of boundaries.

Natural features are not the only basis upon which a boundary may be drawn. Boundaries are made between peoples by differences of language, religion or race as well as by ways of making a living. Europe has many states, partly because she has many physical features which serve as boundaries, but there are more cultures in Europe than there are natural regions. For example, in that natural region known as the Baltic plain there are Germans, Poles, Lithuanians, Latvians and Estonians. Between these people there are no natural features to serve as boundaries and yet because of racial differences these people are divided.

Let us take one post-war boundary, the western limit of Russia. Hubbard * described this accurately.

"The western boundary of Russia lies on the land, and on plains at that, all the way from the Black Sea to the Arctic Ocean. To be sure, it crosses Lake Ladoga for a few miles between Finland and Russia and Lake Peipus on the Estonia frontier, and it follows the Dniester and other streams in places; but the boundary

* George Hubbard, "The Geography of Europe," 1937, pp. 483-484.

nowhere has any real defense or barrier value except where it crosses the Pripet marshes in southern White Russia. It is an ethnic line established in large part by climate and type of land utilization. On the Dniester the boundary sets Bessarabia into Rumania, much to the annoyance of Russia, for there are about as many Slavs between the Prut and Dniester rivers as there are Rumanians. This is the only Russian border that has caused much friction since the establishment of modern Russia, and until 1936 it bristled with arms and resounded with tramp of double patrol most of the time.

"The Polish-Russian boundary might well be a source of trouble, for it is so drawn as to leave many Russians on the Polish side, not only Ukrainians, who do not mind being out of Russia, but also great blocks of White Russians north of Minsk, as well as many very backward Slavs, who are unprogressive and are a drag on Poland. Still the line is well within the Poland of pre-partition days.

"Between the lands of Latvia and Estonia and those of Russia, the frontier line crosses glaciated plains with no reference to physical features save sections of waterways, but it closely follows ethnic lines and has been in large measure satisfactory. Between Finland and Russia it separates Finno-Ugrians, putting large blocks of Karelians in Russia who would gladly have been with their relatives, the Finns. In fact, Russia has patrolled many miles of this border to prevent Karelian defection from the Soviet cause. The reason for establishing so non-ethnic a line here is Russia's need for the railroad running from Leningrad to the ice-free Arctic harbor on Kola Bay; therefore Finns and Karelians were separated instead of Karelians and Slavs. Karelians are much nearer the Russian level of culture and living standards than they are the Finnish. They were more completely Russianized than the Finns and have not shared to any great extent the aspirations of the Finns."

The treaties of Paris were drawn up with the intention of preventing further trouble. The new boundaries made toward that end were determined in various ways. A few were on the basis of physical geography. Thus they included in a political unit the whole of the territory up to the crest of the natural divide. This was not so much because of a recognition of a geographical philosophy as it was a question of defense. It was on this basis that Italy was granted territory up to the crest of the Tirolean Alps.

And boundaries were drawn on the basis of racial characteristics. Ignoring natural physical conditions, which in the long run cannot be ignored, lines were drawn so as to divide races like Poles from Germans, always difficult. Along the Polish-German borders, for example, the greater numbers were Polish farmers, but penetrating into Polish country were middle class commercial men and professionals who were Germans.

They were in places in the minority but they were most important in the economic life of the region.

Out of the chaos emerged many new or reconstructed political entities: Finland, Latvia, Lithuania, Estonia, Poland, Czechoslovakia, Hungary, Austria and Yugoslavia. Generally, these were ethnic units without regard to economic stability. Germany, densely populated and highly industrial, with not the best of soils, was shorn of food lands, industrial areas and iron ore; her economics were unbalanced. Czechoslovakia was the only new country with a reasonable variety and quantity of resources, but it, as we know, unfortunately contained 3,500,000 Germans, consolidated on the German border.

The complex was so chaotic that, of course, it was impossible to mend by the patching method. Perhaps the war did not go far enough. Perhaps there should have been more revolutions. In addition to the Russian Revolution there was the reversal of Czech loyalty. The German mutiny resulted in the Weimar Republic. The Hungarians had their fling, and there was even an abortive revolution in the French army of which the French do not like to talk. If, on the other hand, there had been a complete reshuffling of the deck, as during the historic French Revolution, we might have seen the disappearance of ethnic and geographic isolation. We might have evolved a United States of Europe.

The French Revolution came about in part because of the inequality of the physical provincialism. Reorganized France completely ignored the provinces. The entire country was divided into *departments*. To have federated the states of Europe and broken up the physical provinces into little political entities under a centralized control is an idea too utopian to be reasonable. Provincialisms, conflicting and divergent, were too strongly fixed upon the people. Provincialisms, objective and subjective, have so entrenched themselves that *any* peace treaty in the nature of things could be no more than an unsatisfactory compromise. The treaties of Paris, as we now well know, set the conditions not of a permanent peace but of the next struggle. The Treaty of Versailles gave Hitler an outline with which to write a program. The geography of Europe is by nature a geography of conflict of divergent aims.

Chapter Fifteen

THE REALISM OF

AUTARKY

Adolph Hitler has done so thorough a job of condemning the Versailles treaty that there is little left for me to say. The treatment of the defeated was so efficacious in placing barriers between nations that programs of living were evolved which were national rather than international. There came to be an intensification of the theory of autarky. Autarky stands for economic independence and self-sufficiency; it is *de*volutionary. It is a tenet of totalitarianism and a declaration of war. It calls for a belief in national superiority but, paradoxically, it is a defense mechanism.

It adjusts the peace-time standard of living to a war-time basis.

It is not new. Every war which involved blockade has moved people toward autarky. It was a familiar device of every nineteenth-century statesman who was economically-minded. It has been neglected by Americans because they had no need for it. Providence has endowed the United States with an almost complete autarky, which in our political terminology is represented by such phrases as "splendid isolation," "immigration quota" and "protective tariff."

In these days of complicated industry for most countries autarky is difficult to achieve. The manufacture of a telephone or an automobile calls for a far-flung commerce. The foreign trade involved in the manufacture of Mazda lamps requires feldspar from Norway, China clay and barites from England, potash from Germany, cork, sienna and raw umber from Mediterranean countries, chromium and manganese from Russia, gum Arabic and sodium carbonate from Africa, nitrates from South America, titanium and bismuth from Australia, damar gum and tin from Malay, and wolframite from Japan. Persia, where they once worshiped the god called Mazda, is about the only region not called upon. We could, under a system of autarky, produce many of these commodities at home, but only with an extra production expense or by sacrificing quality. Autarky seldom means quality; it stands more for cultural isolation, stagnation, and a lowering of the essentials.

Autarky is more nearly achieved through natural endowments in the United States, the British Empire and the Union of Socialistic Soviet Republics than elsewhere. The British Empire is not continuous, which explains the British navy. The U.S.S.R. is so landbound that it has difficulty maintaining contacts with those mineral and tropical regions by which it can satisfy its requirements. Germany and Italy, challenging the world by their axis association, have worried quietly about autarky. Italy is far from achievement, but what about Germany?

Germany, her back to the wall, economically speaking, was in sore straits under the Weimar Republic. One of Hitler's dramatic goals was an approach to independence as a measure of defense. The 25,000,000 souls that represent the increase of population between 1871 and 1911 were fed largely on the basis of manufactures for foreign trade. The truth is that Germany, acre for acre, has not the fertile soil of many of her neighbors, so the Germans were leaders in the development of soil chemistry and the application of fertilizers; they had to be. Germany could not feed herself. Enemies and the circumstances of the world economic disaster prevented Germany from obtaining food by competing in the world industrial market. Something had to be done, and autarky was one possible answer.

In 1938 Germany was self-sufficient in the matter of

beet sugar and potatoes.* There were lacks in wheat, rye, barley, oats, grapes and hops. There were produced sufficient, or almost sufficient, quantities of milk, beef, veal, pork and horse. There was enough tallow, cheese, and bacon fat, but deficiencies in butter and lard, and there were no vegetable oils or fats. To maintain milk, meats, animal fats and oils, it was necessary to import fodders, ground feeds and oil cakes. Of course, sufficiency depends upon the standard of living. The percentage of food sufficiency has been raised in Germany by food substitutes, by changes in diet, and by lowering the standard of living.

Let us consider other essentials. In mineral fertilizers Germany had surpluses. She was a chief source of potash, and had nitrates and phosphates. Her cattle culture was important because of the manures, and she had a coal surplus which she was able in normal times to barter for French or Swedish iron ores, having locally but one-fourth of the necessary iron ore. In 1938 Germany imported one million tons of coffee, and over 200,000 tons of lead came from foreign sources, as well as one-half the consumed zinc. Petroleum production was slight. Of the essential aluminum, manganese, tungsten, antimony, tin and mercury there was none. Cotton and rubber, of course, had a more tropical source, and even wool was largely imported.

* This analysis is from the work of Clarence Heskett, graduate student at Ohio State University. The facts were true *before* the conquests of 1940.

Germany recently claimed for herself a ninety-percent self-sufficiency. Making allowances for wishful thinking and for propaganda, Germany nevertheless made a surprising approach to complete autarky. A hectare is 2½ acres, and Germany within her boundaries recently added 300,000 hectares to her tillable acreage, though at the same time she subtracted 200,000 hectares for defense along the West Wall.

The following is a dispatch from the New York *Times:*

"Berlin, Nov. 4, 1939 (AP).—Germany has stored 8,600,000 tons of wheat and rye against the day when the Reich may be forced by the war to fall back upon a reserve.

"Nazis assert that they will not have to use this supply because of grain shipments received from the Balkans via the Danube River, and their own home-grown harvests. In fact, they say the reserve supply will be built up at the rate of 800,000 tons a year.

"Germany's annual consumption of wheat and rye is more than 7,000,000 tons. The reserve thus insures more than a year's complete supply should all harvests and imports fall, it was pointed out.

"Germany's food situation also was expected to be aided considerably by the acquiring of large areas in potato growing Poland. Potatoes are one of the Reich's main staples and are grown in large quantities in Germany and the territory she has acquired in Poland's dismemberment."

This storage of food is, of course, an acknowledgment of the failure of self-sufficiency.

German housewives were advised to serve apple tea by the official German news agency. In admonishing the populace to preserve apple skins, the agency asserted:

"Fresh skins, which of course must be free from rotton spots, should be placed on a stove with just enough water to cover them and boiled until soft. Then this liquid is passed through a sieve and sweetened according to taste. This apple tea is a delicious hot drink for supper. What remains in the strainer can then be fed to the pigs."

Goats have gained favor in the Nazi regime because they can live on garbage, and yield more milk and cheese in proportion to their weight than a cow. Rabbits also are popular because they live on greens and garbage. The Ministry of Agriculture has pointed out it was nothing short of a crime to kill female rabbits for eating purposes when they could still be used for breeding. The skins of all rabbits killed were ordered delivered to the government, cleaned and dried, not more than twenty-one days after the killing.

Hitler's thesis of Pan-Germany was sentimental. His attitude towards minorities cannot be supported by Americans. But his need, in the name of the German people, to solve their economic problem was realistic. One can argue, as I do, against economic nationalism and against conquest and war. Hitler argues for them.

Though man does not live by bread alone, the staff of life is fundamental. The Germans claimed that they did not have enough to eat, or enough of the comforts of life, which by the standards of *any* idealist is not justice. Let us try to assume the point of view of the militant German nationalist before the outbreak of hostilities.

Any student of economics will realize that the Austro-Hungarian Empire was economically logical. It brought together mountain and plains so that they might contribute to each other. It gave the interior a sea coast on the Adriatic. Industrial area traded with rural area. But this economic empire was broken up by the treaties, countries were cut away from the whole and swaddled in defensive tariff barriers. Austria was merely the left-over remnant of six million people, many of them living in mountainous regions, and there were 2,000,000 in Vienna. Vienna, once the capital of an empire, was top heavy. It was with certain logic, as well as his sentimental idea, that Hitler started out to bring all Germans, and perhaps all old Austria-Hungary, under one rule. With the logic of need, he began to acquire new lands with additional or different resources. And there remains the still-unfulfilled logic that the economics of central Europe would be improved by unity. So Hitler apparently thought. His program had originally three aims. He would, and has, removed the conditions of the Versailles Treaty. He would, and largely has, brought contiguous Germans under one rule. He desires to acquire more and different natural resources so that his Germans can live better.

Let us examine the resources he acquired before the invasion of Poland. Austria had but 32,000 square miles and 6,700,000 souls.* A large portion of the country was alpine and sub-alpine, waste or productive only of forests. Eliminating these, the population of usable lands in Austria was about 400 persons to the square mile. Austria has twice the area of Switzerland, yet the land cannot support twice the people. The following facts are from Hubbard's recent study of Europe.†

	Switzerland	Austria
Area in square miles	16,000	32,000
Population	4,000,000	6,700,000
Industrial workers	46 %	40%
Forest	22.7%	37%
Waste	28 %	10%
Grassland	20 %	23%
Water power available	3,000,000 h.p.	1,700,000 h.p.
Water power used	1,000,000 h.p.	700,000 h.p.

Austria produced in 1929 some 3,525,000 tons of coal; Switzerland produced none. So Austria had only the dubious advantages of more coal and less waste land. The absorption of Austria by the German Reich gave

* Austria has 210 persons to the square mile. Ohio has 121. And yet a large proportion of Austria is forest or alpine wasteland. Ohio has complete trade communications with adjacent regions and the sea. Austria has neither.

† George D. Hubbard, "Geography of Europe," 1937, p. 686.

Germany no great advantage. The country was suffering from overpopulation under an enforced economic nationalism, so it supplied no foodstuffs to Germany. There were huge salt resources and salt is basic in many chemical industries, but Germany was not without its own salt resources. However, the modest reserve of Austrian iron ore was welcome.

Czechoslovakia was a better prize. Of all the countries of Europe it had the best economy. But it lacked communication to the sea. Access to world commerce was largely through German Hamburg, for the Elbe is navigable all the way to Prague. On the other hand, railways crossed the boundaries in sixty-five places, and for 100 miles the international Danube River formed a national limit.

Essentially there were three physical provinces in Czechoslovakia; the Bohemian platform, the Moravian corridor, and the Slovakian piedmont. The Bohemian region consists of low plateau and lowland guarded by an arc of low wooded mountains on the west, north, and south, and marked on the south by the Danube. On the plateau grow wheat, rye and oats, potatoes and flax, and the farms support cattle and hogs. Hops have made brewing at Budweis and Pilsen famous, and clean sand accounts for the Bohemian glass. Coal and iron ore make Kladno a manufacturing center. The list of manufactures at Prague is imposing. The Bohemian lowlands are even more fertile than the uplands. Grain, potatoes (industrial alcohol), and beets (sugar) support mills and refineries; hops are exported to Germany; ninety percent of the region is agricultural. There is more glass there, and they make porcelain, china, beads, paper, textiles and lesser metal products.

The Moravian corridor between the Bohemian mountains and the Carpathians is at once agricultural and commercial. The transportation facilities encourage industry. The Slovak mountain area does not have the industrial significance of the rest of the late Czechoslovakia. It and Carpathian Ruthenia are rustic, supporting an important animal culture. Germany had less claim here, and little ethnic affinity.

According to Hubbard, the country of Czechoslovakia as a whole had of all Austria-Hungarian industry in 1914:

83%	*of the coal*
60%	*of the iron and steel mills*
75%	*of the cotton mills*
85%	*of the hemp mills*
44%	*of the glass works*
80%	*of the woolen mills*
95%	*of the sugar mills*

How important are these resources to Germany? Czechoslovakia was importing food from the more southern countries, and had no great excess of food to give to Germany. But her economic status raised somewhat the German standard of living. Also, it provided more trade and industry within the territory of the German mark. It added 3,000,000 Germans to the

Reich, more soldiers, as well as eleven million other, less willing citizens. It gave Germany one of the world's greatest munition works and the largest shoe factory. If Czechoslovakia did not add greatly to autarky it made plausible a further imperialism.

Are the former German colonies worth fighting for? They were numerous and scattered but not large except for East and Southwest Africa. Though not exactly coincident, consider the statistics for Tanganyika as representing East Africa. There is a native population today of 5,138,000 persons, plus 8,455 whites. Tanganyika produces cotton at the rate of 56,500 bales (1936-37) and can produce more; Germany in 1936 imported 1,092,000 bales. The other significant production is a modest amount of antimony, much needed by Germany. Southwest Africa is less important except that it produces half the world's supply of vanadium, which of itself is hardly worth fighting for. However one may deprecate the value of the colonies, Great Britain and France have not the least inclination to surrender them to Germany or Italy. Also, though colonial products can be bought in the open market, political control brings both product and market within the currency exchange of the mother country.

Well, autarky is difficult to achieve. And it is an expression of fear, a sign that something is very wrong. I am still wondering about Belgium's solution of the food problem; Belgium cannot feed itself. It is the most densely populated country in Europe, with few indus-

trial resources though it is a most industrialized country. Of all the countries in the world it has the largest
volume of foreign trade per capita; it buys and sells
in the open market. How many trade restrictions are
due to national psychologies of fear and aloofness?
Perhaps the first remedy for a trend toward the stagnation of culture is a standardized currency. Gold has
practically no value, really, so we assign it a value, and
other countries give it other values. Already a large
proportion of the gold in the world has been stored
in a hole in the ground in Kentucky. Why not suppose
that *all* the gold were collected in that hole, and given
a definite value. Then we could issue an international
currency on the basis of that value. Certainly that
would simplify international economics.

This chapter on autarky is written from the point
of view of geographic realism. I sympathize with the
simplicity of any geographic economy which would
permit one central European political entity. And I see
certain justification for a Mediterranean singleness of
purpose. But remember that I have political morals in
weighing grim realities, though I may remain silent
upon them. I do not condone the political, the often
stupid, domination of minorities. I see virtue in economic unity of purpose but this does not require the
suppression of civil and political rights.

Of course, the difficulty in any co-operation lies in
diverging psychologies; that was the justification for
my previous discussion of the subject. A Baltic gentle-

man writing to an American friend remarked: "You
know from the conversations which I had the pleasure
of having with you two years ago that I look with considerable skepticism on the materialistic philosophy and
on its results both in learning and in ethics. It is not
possible to understand the real essence of either European or even German and Italian affairs, and least of
all Polish or Baltic ones without properly appreciating
the spiritual forces which, hidden to the eyes of a foreign observer, play a decisive role in the collective life
of various nations. We cannot explain or estimate in
figures this moral force in nations which preserve their
entity and are ready to suffer the greatest sacrifices for
the preservation and perfection of their language and
their native culture and for the freedom to cultivate
their own land." He goes on to explain that this idea
is foreign to Americans because theirs is "a civilization
of a mechanised land and materialistic existence." We
do have difficulty in understanding, but for a different
reason. We are not so bound to soil and locale and are
consequently less in harmony with our environment;
we do not have the peasant consciousness. And socially
we are an agglomeration of people who denied the
bonds of race by the very act of migration; we will
never form as a people a "pure" race. Proud of being
not a single metal but an alloy, our virtue partly lies
in our diversity of origin. Furthermore, we are peace-
loving simply because we possess almost everything we

need. We do not need the word "autarky" in our lexicon. As we are by origin various we are international in outlook and sympathies. Our response to world-wide stimuli, and our development of far-flung commercial contacts are the very leaven of our civilization.

Chapter Sixteen

NATIONAL CONSERVATION

IS SOCIALISM

In this short volume the reader has been informed many times that history is but a series of provincial stories, and that civilization is a kaleidoscopic pattern of provincial colorings. The color of a provincial culture depends upon the character of the local earth stuff from which man builds, upon man's cultural inheritance and, lastly, upon the invention and ingenuity of the local group. In primitive societies provinces were small, and the culture was limited by a valley, a moor or a coastal plain. In later feudal days the provincialisms were represented by greater territory. We had Brittany to contrast with Normandy; Leon against Navarre. With the modern period there came into existence competing nationalisms, which were political provincialisms held together by geographic circumstance or artificial restraint. It may be in this year of writing that we are approaching an era of even greater territorial unity, for struggles are being waged for Pan-Asia and Pan-Europe. But it is unwise to forecast.

We live in a political provincialism known as the United States of America. It is an association of provinces of many hues. The dreamy blue haze of the southern Appalachians is unlike the tawny landscape of the California valley. Mellow New England with its fine adjustment of man to meadow has little in common with the rawness of the scene in central Georgia. There is within our borders corn land and spruce forest, cotton land and areas of mill and grimy stack. Different as these are, by sea and by circumstance they are bound together in that whole we call our nation. And by their richness and their variety they have served us well—indeed, they have served us too well. The prodigal offering of resource has created in us a character-wrecking philosophy of plenty, and left us with an unjustified expectancy of continuing, unlimited wealth, whence comes our policy of *laissez-faire,* our rampant individualism, and our opposition to the obvious social advantages of much recent legislation. We know, of course, that the Chinese were wasteful of their forests in past ages and now must carefully conserve. We understand, if vaguely, Germany's problem of *lebensraum*, and even justify Britain's imperialism as an expression of realism. Yet we find it hard to apply these experiences to our future. We look to some divine intervention to save us from parallel catastrophes. America is the physician who can cure the world but knows not its own ills. Even if it hurts our nationalism, let us now be realistic about ourselves.

It is not simple for a patriot to write wisely and dispassionately of his own country. Foreigners like James Bryce and André Siegfried saw us most clearly. A native needs perspective. The expatriot returning to his homeland reacts more sensitively than one who remained among the familiar. Louis Adamic wrote his beautiful "Native's Return" only after a long American experience, and my brother Donald wrote the essentially American "A Prairie Grove" after residence in France, though his best picture of the American continent is found in "Green Laurels." One paragraph runs:

"This is the continent I sing, not ours by a million years, not named, one of the six great blocks of the world, the most intemperate, with heartwood the hardest. For ages without number it stood grandly, indifferently empty of men. While Asia was filling with humans and human debris, it was still empty of them, the sun shining on the grass in the valley, the night finding beasts in the forest. It was full already with roots in the soil and armies of birds sweeping northward, going southward; it was already perfection; nothing in it knew lack."

And yet in these three hundred years we have spread our human pest over the continent and far advanced the land's despoliation. We have plowed cruel strips, and mined out scars, we have polluted air and stream, and man-made sores fester on the landscape. Learn how tree and grass have died from smelter fumes about Butte, Montana. Read about the hideous erosion of the hills about Ducktown, Tennessee. Observe the ugliness and squalor of the tenement district in any New England cotton town. And if you have compassion enough and a not too great love of nature, visit the West Virginia mining communities.

Despite our obvious failures to preserve the beauty and wealth of the continent, there is no American school system but teaches that we are the greatest people on earth. Well, we are still the richest, but our most distinguishing trait is that we are also the most wasteful. One foreigner called us a nation of butchers. For too long we have eaten at a plentiful table and our refuse can has held far more than we have consumed. It is this consumption and waste that should form the theme of any true study of American geography. Today we have taken up that theme seriously and call the study conservation. Textbooks have proudly indicated the high position of the United States in the production of this commodity or that. Now the same books are beginning to show our country as it is, first in wastefulness, with ever-divergent curves of demand and supply. There are those who have long known this and tried to warn us, but it takes time to educate one hundred million people. Nevertheless we are being brought to a sense of our wastefulness. Perhaps it was war and the preparedness for war that awakened us. But the United States seems to have lost that splendid isolation with which certain verbose statesmen would endow it. The ramifications of our economic system lead us into foreign countries hungry for our resources, and we have been forced to realize that our resource wealth makes us a leader among nations, and that our waste weakens that same leadership.

But we have a greater reason for putting our house in order. That is to raise our standard of living. We must make more careful, more intelligent adjustment of our lives to our earth as we find it. Perhaps the Calvinists were right when they thought of frugality as next to Godliness. Moreover, beyond the humanitarian aspect lies the defense of our democracy against open or insidious attack. Ideas foreign to our order find fertile ground among us, not only among the intellectually discontented, but more particularly among those living on meager and sub-economic incomes, such as our low-paid white-collar workers, the farmer on relief, the border-line shopkeeper, W.P.A. workers, and share croppers. We need a contented nation, well-fed, well-clothed, well-housed and participating in happiness. There still remains enough wealth to go around for we have not *yet* wasted all of our abundance. It is only our faulty adjustment to earth conditions, our poverty of geographic intelligence, that is at fault.

Of course, in a country such as the United States, our economic problems are huge and varied. Theorists talk of solution in terms of increased consumption, shorter hours and deficit financing. We are pulled first this way and then that by the economists: "We are wondering. We don't know!" But of this we can be certain: we have spent our incomes and gone into our principal like drunkards. That is poor geography. We must increase geographic knowledge until every citizen understands the limitations of the budget imposed upon him by circumstance. By democratic processes, we must impose spending restrictions upon our citizens until such time as we can expect him to undertake the responsibility of living within his natural budget. Such an imposition is called national conservation, and the assumption of responsibility by the citizenry will be, one supposes, a sort of millennium.

As it is, we have almost killed the goose that laid the golden eggs. The government is showering us with warnings that tell us that 97 percent of the Great Plains has suffered undue erosion, and that 50 percent is impoverished. In one year we wasted more coal than was needed to satisfy the entire wants of Germany. Yet this characteristic wastefulness is not only American; it is not peculiar to us alone. It springs from a naïve weakness found in all humanity faced with abundance; it

is a basic, new-land psychology. But now that resources
are failing (the copper taken from the earth cannot be
replaced, and much of our first-class coal is gone), the
psychology which condones waste must be set aside.
This is especially true in the face of an expanding
population, and our new technological needs.

The first public consciousness of dwindling resources
was in the case of our timber. The original forests of
the United States spread over almost half the country
in unbroken expanse, some 900,000,000 acres, more than
500 varieties of trees. For miles there was but one type
of tree; elsewhere a hundred varieties inhabited one
square mile, white pine 200 feet tall, oaks nine feet in
diameter, and unbelievably large sequoias. We cleared
forests for fields, cut trees for fuel and for timber, and
burned them through carelessness. And still we annually burn on the stump more trees than we cut. So, of
that original forest area, there remains but half, and
most of that is inferior.

As early as President Harrison's administration, timber lands were withdrawn from sale for private use,
but the first dramatic step in our forest preservation was
taken by the energetic Theodore Roosevelt. By nature
a social revolutionist, he said that national resources,
particularly trees, belonged not to the individual but
to the nation. This, of course, was out-and-out socialism.
The movement for forest preservation grew rapidly
until, in 1911, the Weeks Law was passed, giving
authority to the government to purchase by condemna-

tion forest lands to be preserved for posterity. More than 3,000,000 acres were thus acquired with no objections except from some forest owners. Few people saw the far-reaching social implications of this condemnation of private property for the public good.

Every revolutionary movement has its theorizers who offer justification. The best of the men to explain conservation was Ely, who said, "Conservation, narrowly and strictly considered, means the preservation in unimpaired efficiency of the resources of the earth. . . ." He also urged an increased efficiency, showing how a forest properly managed may increase its output to two and three times that of a wild forest. And efficient adaptation of resources is good geography, for good geography is the study of good living. Ely painted a hopeful picture of the cycle of resource economics: a country is despoiled of its natural wealth, conservation is inevitably forced upon the people, and the result is that a balance is struck between human consumption and national production, except, of course, in the exploitive industries like mining. Old World Asia serves as an example. The question of how to balance consumption and production before our resources are entirely depleted, and how to provide for increasing standards of living, brings Ely to the danger that lies in the conservationists' wish to reduce private income below a fair return in order that a surplus may be reserved for public use. This, of course, is essentially the conflict between individualism and socialism. The answer must be a compromise, but it is safe to say that if progress is to be made, each compromise must, in the nature of things, be nearer the social left.

Conservation is definitely a challenge to the fee simple concept of property rights. The conservationists (geographers) wish, to offset further waste, to control water-power resources, minerals and even soil. From one point of view they are right, but our social order cannot be so suddenly changed without violent revolution for, historically, a democracy is a middle-class government in which private right is sacred. Also, to assume public control of private property is not simple. For example, the government has taken control of certain water rights for irrigation. Farmers are allowed to possess land privately and can expect sufficient water for irrigation. But this balancing of public and private rights is one of the most difficult problems of the Department of Agriculture. Far more than a legal problem, it is one in political economy.

But enough of economic and social theory! The trouble with much of our thought on conservation is that our literature on the subject is almost devoid of discussion of the dollar. Both the English and the French have the same curious lack. One Frenchman said, "Economics is not eager for facts." German thought has been more realistic, for conservation has long been a part of the *Kultur*.

Nor is all conservation good. The sentimentalists may so tie up our resources as to be wasteful. They would preserve Niagara Falls in its entirety for the pleasure of honeymoon couples, preventing its use for water power. Every community has this problem. Shall it preserve shade trees, or cut them down to make room for necessary traffic lanes? Only God can make a tree, but if more farm land is needed forests must go. Production is only wasteful if the total cost of production is greater than the return. The difficulty is that the relation between man and his resources is not constant, nor is there any steady, directional change in values. What is economical for one period may prove false economy in terms of the decade or century.

This uncertainty of values and relative values becomes most evident when discussing sub-marginal land. There is no such thing inherently as sub-marginal land, but there is a temporary sub-marginal state when productivity of land, cost of transportation, market price and many other things combine to create temporarily a hazardous economy. The Dust Bowl has sub-marginal economics today only if farmed by the methods used in the days of its prosperity. In 1890 this land was good to look upon. Over broad acres grass waved knee-high, the land sold for a dollar an acre. Even by crude farming methods the land gave every promise of profit. But the climate changed, the people plowed too deep and too extensively, and the price of farm products dropped. In 1934 even catastrophic China could pity us. Dust storms, terrible and heart-rending, raged over the Great Plains. Violent black winds blotted out sun and stars.

Trees were smothered. Men died of grief as much as from starvation. Yet I would not have the courage to mark the area of the Great Plains as sub-marginal on a map because it might be otherwise before the map was published. Climate may change, price may change or conservation methods may reclaim the drifting dust, as they have done and are doing.

I have a story from Vermont that I like. Government agents tried to move a hill farmer from his land because they claimed it was sub-marginal. But it was not sub-marginal to him for it paid excellent dividends: he stayed because he said he liked the view. There is a more significant story from Texas, which illustrates the importance of intelligent adaptation of land to purpose. It is significant because it shows no conflict between socialistic conservation, and the processes of democracy. The region had been blasted by the withering climate. In one dead tree crows lacking other materials used barbed wire to build themselves a nest. Yet this territory today supports cover crops which hold the dust in place, and slowly but surely the ground water level is being raised. What men saw as the task of a decade or two has been accomplished in three years. New practices of contour plowing and ditching now protect the region from any such complete erosion in the future.

Prosperity has been forced back into the area by a communal effort directed by the government, and each inhabitant is now conscious of a social philosophy. The government accomplished its ends by education and not by dictation, an example of social democracy at its best. Conservation was practiced here not because of a theory but because it demonstrated to the community that it would pay. In some cases in the west even the die-hard public utilities are giving definite support to this new socialism, for you cannot sell electric power to an impoverished farmer.

Individualism and selfishness do not pay. Conservation calls for collective intelligence and for co-operation. Katherine Glover in her excellent "America Begins Again" tells of a dramatic failure by quoting from two authors who were describing Stewart County in Georgia. The first quotation is from Margaret Mitchell's "Gone With The Wind," presenting spring in Georgia, with fertile fields smiling up "to a warm sun, placid, complacent, at their edges the virgin forests." Then a quotation from Stuart Chase's "Rich Land, Poor Land." He visited the same counties with their "shacks for farmhouses, bleak unpainted churches, deserted lumber mills, rickety cotton gins." He describes the gullies for which Stewart County is now infamous, begun by an unguarded trickle from a barn, and continued until there were red gashes in the soil, some a hundred yards across. In that one county 40,000 acres were destroyed. Countless tons of dirt ran away to clog up the streams. But the real fault lies in a political system which refused to heed or regulate the acts of individuals, a political system founded upon the mistaken philosophy of inexhaustible resources.

Socialism does not mean dictatorship. Advancement towards conservation and good living in the Tennessee Valley, our greatest experiment in better living, is not a function of governmental insistence but of voluntary co-operation on the part of the majority of the people. Understand this clearly, for the government by new social theories is not forcing people to conserve resources. Depletion of resources is forcing people to new social theories. The government is merely an agent of the people, in this case, an educational agent.

In the Texas area just described there were certain people who refused governmental advice, and now those people are living shabby lives in the midst of prosperity. In new public work projects there may be those who by right of eminent domain are evicted from their homes, and so are discontented. But this does not change the fact that the greatest good for the greatest number is a democratic principle. The new geography, conservation, is not man's adaptation of the earth to his individual purpose. It is the intelligent, long-range use of natural resources for the needs of a group and their descendants. It is a planned economy, which must eliminate false economics and disregard the selfish rights of the individual. National conservation is socialism.

Chapter Seventeen

THE GEOGRAPHY

OF PEACE

I HAVE TRIED TO WRITE A BOOK ABOUT THE PROGRESS OF man, how, tilling the soil and sailing ships, he has gradually come intelligently to bend this earth more and more to his purpose. I have tried to say little about kings and the wars they wage. But, alas, men have made so sorry a mess of their own story that one might have entitled this little volume "From Stone Ax to Dive Bomber."

Yet I would do an injustice to my wishful thinking and my essentially optimistic philosophy were I not to offer my manifesto on what peace might be and how it could come into being. War-conscious readers will smile at my naïveté, and the futility of my offering. But we will never have peace until we insist on thinking about it. Man needs no intelligence to start a war. Yet he is called upon for his greatest intelligence if he can hold to peace. This is true because peace, if it is not an abstraction, is at least intangible. There is nothing glittering or splendid about it. Many men do not believe in it or hope for its permanent attainment. When we say that peace is merely the interval between wars, or that in time of peace one should prepare for war, we acknowledge ourselves as defeatists. Though my personal ideas as to the stuff of peace may be considered Utopian, I must have my say in order to stand apart from those fatalists who see war as a biological essential of culture.

My philosophy of history is that great leaders, politicians and reformers are but interludes. Most histories are sequences of man-made events which we have difficulty in remembering because of their essentially temporary character. Most history is the story, not of man's progress, but of man's mistakes. The continuity in the long story of man is the environmental scene. Governments have changed many times in France, but the Frenchman continues to be a tiller of the soil, a specialist of the cabbage patch. Russia has given up weak tsar for strong dictator, and still the Volga River, like a wise old snake, knows more about Russia than all the political theorists in the world. Mountains must smile at the wars men wage about them. It is the fertility of the soil or its barrenness, the storms of a sea or the water's placidity, the seclusion of a forest retreat or the freedom of an open range, that really marks the mind of man. It is the everlasting earth that gives us the theme for our scenario. And so if we are to forecast a utopian world where war is no longer necessary, we must not invent a new political theory. We must look to a better adjustment of men to the earth's bounty, and a better distribution of the necessities of life.

It is generally conceded that wars in this modern day are fundamentally economic. I know that men fight because of differences in ideals, and because of some psychological divergence, but I hope that I have shown in previous chapters that not a few of these differences arise from economic provincialisms. If war has an economic basis, then peace in the place of strife will have to be an economic solution of world problems. What is fundamentally wrong with the world, except for the persistent inhumanity of humans, is distribution and man's inability to redistribute.

To begin with, centers of population and sources of necessities do not coincide. Tremendous numbers of men live in the region of coal mines. They mine coal and they make iron and steel and machines and gadgets. Yet the coal and steel and gadgets are not edible. Man cannot free himself from the tilled field, and masses of men in industrial centers of population must assure themselves free access to wheat though it take the entire British navy to do so.

Men have done something in the way of distribution. Chosen (Korea) is a small country. Yet before the Japanese took over, there could be a plentiful harvest in the north and starvation in the south. This is now equalized by better transportation. The English in India brought water by canal to irrigate dry lands where thousands starved in periods of drought. In America we supplement our dwindling meat supply with Argentine beef, and when eggs are short in New York City a ship will come into port bearing a million foreign eggs.

This is the story of commercial geography. But there is no equality. It is every nation for itself. Koreans may be fed by the Japanese, but immediately across the border in Siberia men are still hungry. "From him that hath not shall be taken away even that which he hath." The spoils still go to the victor.

International law is merely a set of usages to be subscribed to if convenient and profitable. Actually, international relations approach anarchy. The world is competitive. We cut prices until it is no longer profitable, and then we cut throats. At the end of the war there is a peace founded on compromise, and the treaty is merely a setting forth of the conditions of the next war. In the opinion of the writer, if the next peace is to last more than ten years it *must* make sound geographic sense.

A fundamental cause of the last two wars has been territorial. In some cases the territory was adjacent, and in other cases it was colonial. Possession of territory means opportunity for capitalistic expansion, markets in which trade can be carried on under the special monetary system of the exploiters. So, it is not really territory for which men struggle, but the right to the produce thereof. It is the right to buy and sell in an open market without political restriction that counts. There is no lack of *Lebensraum*. There is only a faulty system of distribution. The Brazilians dump coffee into the sea when the surplus endangers the world price. In the little Vermont village where I now write, when we have a fruit surplus, we call in the needy and give it to them.

In the international world potential production of raw materials is unbelievably great, and the world's potential manufactured output far exceeds possible consumption. The failure of modern economics is distribution, and the great barrier to distribution is selfish control. There is nothing wrong with Mother Earth; only man is vile, for man is *so* provincial. He has erected for himself a political system known as nationalism, and he thinks it treason to doubt its virtues. He has stalemated himself by his dogmatic point of view.

To free ourselves we must conceive of social and humanitarian, as well as economic, aspects of trade. We must cast aside the Carthaginian Moloch. Commerce is always something more than a venture with hope of profit. A highway, a railway, a ship route is a leveler, a distributor of equality and civilization. Nothing is more geographic than a route. It is of vast social and economic significance from its beginning as a path between the tea bushes of Assam until it ends in a by-street of the English Midlands, just in time for tea. Trade is good socialism. Isolation and autarky are, from the point of view of world progress, immoral.

Why, then, have we failed to make the advantages of trade equal among men? Why don't we solve the problem of distribution? This failure, I suppose, is partly due to the very complexity of the problem, and partly, mostly, due to a biological greed. We must about-face and realize that political control gives a nation legal possession but not a moral possession of resources. Such a statement is, of course, anti-nationalistic, even unpatriotic, but it belongs to the new realm of internationalism. If this be treason, make the most of it. But remember that the alternative is nationalistic war. Then you must give up butter for cannon, and cannon as offensive weapons can by no rational process be thought of as constructive.

It is good Christianity, or good Buddhism, and would be approved by Confucious, to say that the opportunity to buy at reasonable prices is as much an inalienable right as the pursuit of happiness. If it is true that no individual or nation has a right to a monopoly of surplus when a neighbor suffers from lack, it is equally logical to conceive of some readjustment of national possessions. This is well enough in the abstract, but just try to take some possession from a "have" nation to give it to a "have-not"! Imperialists tremble at the mention of "space for living" by crowded nations. The basic wrong upon this chaotic, globular entity we call the Earth, is the lack of a scheme for *INTERNA-TIONAL* living.

I cannot propose in these last few pages a panacea for our multitude of ills, yet each of us can think of ways of peace at least as easily as we think of ways of war. There should be at least two fundamental postulates for any world-wide international plan. The simplest is an international currency, based upon a single gold reserve, or a silver reserve, or plain common sense. The second postulate is the unified support of some plan for peace by *ALL* the nations of the earth, based upon a sense of humanity, or an abhorrence of war, or a sensible desire for better business. I cannot feel that motives are as important as results. It would seem as if any international plan would at least call for the discarding of export duties on raw materials, and import duties on manufactured goods. This should end all talk of autarky, and abolish the war mongers.

If peace is to be based upon economic adjustment, there is no reason to disturb theories of government, or political boundaries. It is possible to have world economic peace, and yet have the state exist for mankind in one territory, while man exists for the state in the next. Kings, presidents, and local dictators, could equally lay their corner stones, and make addresses over nation-wide hookups. Actually, the world suffers not so much from fear of any change in political ideas as from a fear of a reduction of the standard of living. War is an effort to improve standards of living, that is, war is for booty, but in the long run it must always be entered on the deficit side of the ledger. It might be cheaper to grant some points, to give up a portion of one's resources to a "have-not," than to pay the horrible cost of a war. In this country we only recently finished paying off the bills for the War of 1812!

With an international currency, an abolishment of national tariffs, and universal support for world peace, how are we going to distribute fairly the earth's bounty? Take such a commodity as tin, which is needed universally to preserve food though it is very much localized in production. Tin comes almost exclusively from two areas. The major area is in the region of the Malay Straits, under Dutch and British control. The Dutch control is at the moment questionable, and Japan and the United States are watching each other with green-eyed curiosity as to the future ownership. A second and lesser source is in Bolivia.

To keep nations from fighting for tin it would be logical to apportion the product fairly, according to the needs of each country. Shall we have an international commission charged with the distribution of tin? The private or national owners would then be assured a profit on production. Each nation would pay the same price at the refinery but, of course, would have freight differentials. That takes away no private or political ownership of the metal, but as far as tin goes there would be world-planned distribution, and any nation would be permitted to sell its quota to the highest bidder should it choose to do so. There would also be commissions for iron and copper and manganese, the whole list of essential minerals. Yet each country could live under its own system of private capitalism or state socialism as it pleased. The only political change would be that the advantages of imperialism would gradually diminish.

Considering world control of agricultural production the matter is less simple. It would seem that a nation had a first right to the food it raised, but the exportable surplus should be controlled by an impartial, international commission. Within a country people have a right to food or to revolution. Governments even give food to the needy. It is easy, and perfectly logical, to extend this principle to the world, regardless of national boundaries. On paper, the principle seems almost too obvious, though nationalistic greed prevents its practice except in the case of war relief or major catastrophe.

The commissions for the separate commodities would necessarily be co-ordinated, and there would be a court of final appeal. Should the court have an international police force? Probably. The world would then be controlled by an economic, not a political, League of

Nations. The plan makes geographic sense. Food would be produced where it could best be produced. Manufactures would be developed where those manufactures were logical. Trade would flow evenly to and from the ends of the earth. A cosmopolitanism would exist which would immeasurably advance civilization. There would not be a perfect equality of the standards of living, but one agricultural economy would more nearly match another agricultural economy, and industrial standards of living would everywhere be approximate. However, there still would be opportunity for personal or national initiative and inventiveness. This is not capitalism or communism, for no economic theory is prescribed, but it would be true humanity and good geography.

My economist friends have already taken great pleasure in picking holes in this incomplete, loosely knit scheme. They are adept in discovering what is wrong with the world, and what are the causes of war. They are diagnosticians, but they are not physicians. And I see through a glass but darkly. But I have one conviction to which I hold. That is that we have outgrown provincialisms and national boundaries, and our planned economy in the future, if we are to abolish war, must be worldwide in scope. We are having *forced* upon us a brotherhood of man; leaders in the future will be men with international sympathies.

This brings me to the end of my volume, but not to the end of my work. There are many geographic highways yet to be followed, many byways yet unknown. Geographic ignorance leads to snobbery, intolerance and war. Geographic education leads to the exact opposite. In the nature of things, geography leads to internationalism, and should go on apace until the world is linked:

"From Delos up to Limerick and back."

FURTHER READINGS

No BOOK, nor teacher for all that, can complete the
thought. That has to be done by individual curiosity.
A fact is clinched in one's mind by the direct method
of finding it hidden between the lines of a book. The
reading of a thesis written directly to the point is not
as convincing as a self-made discovery. Hence this partial but suggestive bibliography.

* * * * *

Geographers have many learned discourses on the
history of geography. Rather than these, read the simple

"Theory of Environment" by A. H. Koller, or "The Making of Geography" by Dickinson and Howerth. The environmental theory is pleasantly presented in "Life and Environment" by S. B. Sears. A college text from the environmentalistic viewpoint is my own "New College Geography." A well-written and more modern point of view is found in Preston James' "An Outline of Geography." Read in Brunhes' "Human Geography" (translated by W. Compte and edited by Bowman and Dodge). It is the best illustrated geography. There is an important article, H. H. Barrows' "Geography as Human Ecology," in the *Annals of the Association of American Geographers*. This is a research journal and contains examples of chorography, as does the readable *Geographical Review,* the foremost geographical publication in the world.

Do you lack an atlas? The "Commercial" atlas with railroads and post offices has little literary value. The best atlas in English is the "London *Times* Atlas"— huge and expensive. Buy "Goode's School Atlas," revised edition, which has excellent cartography.

Be discriminating in reading travel books. Some are insincere or superficial. One book on the South Seas was so patently false that I burned it in the furnace. The next week I received a letter from Tahiti condemning it. Others are pure hoaxes. Siberia is the subject of two such impositions. One has an occasional calculated error in order to give the informed a key to the hoax. Another is intended to fool everyone and fools none. Then there is the obnoxious travel writer who was entertained by the officers at Gibraltar, and proceeded to break every rule of code possible as a stunt. Of another sort is the searching and quite excellent "Travels in the Congo" by André Gide. Read the poetic "Old Morocco and the Forbidden Atlas" by the late Clarence E. Andrews, a connoisseur, or Peter Fleming's "News from Tartary" or "One's Company." A most intelligent book is "West of the Pacific" by Ellsworth Huntington. Louis Adamic's "The Native's Return" certainly should be read. Harry Franck has a number of good books. But the most delightful travel book in all the world is Hilaire Belloc's "Path to Rome." Of his many books this presents Belloc at his best; his style is inimitable.

CHAPTER II

The references mentioned for Chapter One are here applicable. A tremendous mass of anthropogeographical material is found in E. C. Semple's "Influences of Geographical Environment." There is a survey in Whitbeck and Thomas's "The Environmental Factor." For criticism of the environmental factor note that most histories ignore it. An exception is Frederick Turner's "Frontier in American History." Other critics are Lucien Febvre's "A Geographical Introduction to History"; C. Daryll Forde's "Habitat, Economy and Society"; and Roland B. Dixon's "The Building of

Culture." They are all men who have little use for environmentalism.

The question of urban geography is discussed in Eugene Van Cleef's "Trade Centers and Trade Routes," and Lewis Mumford's "The Culture of Cities."

CHAPTER IV

There are a number of popular geologies at one's disposal. Fenton's "This Amazing Earth" is excellent. A readable text book in which the life story is clear is Cleland's "Geology."

CHAPTER V

Geography in culture is well represented by A. R. Cowan's "Master Clues in World History"; John Fiske's "Outlines of Cosmic Philosophy," part II, chap. xviii; N. S. B. Gras's "An Introduction to Economic History"; W. M. F. Petrie's "Some Sources of Human History"; and James Fairgrieve's "Geography and World Power." The story of the diffusion of ideas is scattered and most fragmentary. The thesis of environmental screens is treated by Ellsworth Huntington, in "The Character of Races."

If one reads on ancient Egypt one turns first to the works of James Breasted. A book that might escape your attention is L. M. Phillips' "Art and Environment." Miss Boyd's Polish studies are referred to in a footnote. The Saharan oasis of Kufra is treated by Rosita Forbes in "The Secret of the Sahara," and more importantly by A. M. Hassanain's "The Lost Oasis." One gets in the proper spirit for all this by reading the fanciful "Lost Horizon" by James Hilton.

CHAPTER VII

One should begin the study of nomadism with studies from the Bible. Cowan, previously mentioned, is excellent, as are Semple or Fairgrieve. Ellsworth Huntington's "The Pulse of Asia" is good, and there is always Marco Polo, especially "Ser Marco Polo," edited by Cordier. Then there are T. E. Lawrence's "Seven Pillars of Wisdom," Doughty's "Arabia Deserta," and Gertrude Bell's "Letters."

CHAPTERS VII AND IX

The scholarly will discover that much that I wrote came from the chapters on the sea in E. C. Semple's "Influence of Geographic Environment." N. S. Shaler, always delightful, wrote a worthy book called "The Sea and the Land." E. C. Semple's "The Geography of the Mediterranean Region" and Marion Newbigin's "Mediterranean Lands" will give you a picture of the enclosed sea. These volumes aid in understanding the Roman world. Studies of Rome are apt to be ponderous, but any work of Rostovtzeff is delightful for its English alone. The story of English cultural enlargement following the period of exploration is found in W. C. Abbott's "The Expansion of Europe."

CHAPTER X

There are numerous social studies of medieval times, but they ordinarily ignore any geographical factor. The story of climate and the Renaissance is to be found in "Civilization and Climate" by Ellsworth Huntington, or "Climatic Changes" by Huntington and Visher.

CHAPTERS XI AND XII

Here one had best turn from the academic to general literature. Novelists know about psychology; ordinarily geographers do not.

Sheila-Kaye-Smith, *Sussex George*
D. C. Peattie, *A Prairie Grove*
Elizabeth Roberts, *The Great Meadow*
Pearl Buck, *The Good Earth*
Edith Wharton, *Ethan Frome*
Willa Cather, *My Antonia*
Thomas Hardy, *The Return of the Native*
Louis Bromfield, *The Farm*
Mary Austin, *The Land of Little Rain*
Ruth Sandow, *Old Jules*
Julius Halterman, *Dust*
Hamlin Garland, *A Son of the Middle Border*

Neil Gunn, *Morning Tide*
W. H. Hudson, *The Purple Land*
Pierre Loti, *An Iceland Fisherman*
S. O. Jewett, *The Country of the Pointed Firs*
A. B. Green, *The Lone Winter*
Joseph Conrad, *Typhoon*
J. B. Priestly, *English Journey*
Lucy Furman, *The Quare Women*
Robert Frost, *New Hampshire*
Mary Ellen Chase, *A Goodly Heritage*
This, of course, is but a beginning.

THE REMAINDER OF THE BOOK

The readings one should pursue for the remainder of this book are largely in current literature, too numerous to mention. I shall record at length, however, the references on conservation. But there are a few books to which I must call your attention. D. W. Johnson has written "Topography and Strategy in the World War" upon which my material on the war was directly built. Van Valkenburg recently produced a book on the principles of "Political Geography," and Derwent Whittlesey wrote the excellent "The Earth and the State." The geography of the Versailles Treaty is found in Isaiah Bowman's "The New World." Every number of the journal, "Foreign Affairs," is valuable.

For conservation turn to the Library of Congress, Division of Bibliography, a publication "Conservation of Natural Resources; A Selected List of Recent Writings" (free). The same division has available "A List of References on the United States Civilian Conservation Corps." If you wish to learn what one community is doing in conservation education, send to the Department of Conservation Education, Zanesville, Ohio, Public Schools.

An important step in conservation was the publication of "Conservation of Natural Resources" by C. R. Van Hise. A modern version of the Van Hise material is to be found in the volume edited by Parkins and Whitaker (revised edition 1939), "Our Natural Resources and Their Conservation." It is an excellent, factual book in which economics and sociology appear largely by implication. To me the most provocative book was published in 1920. This is by Ely, Hess, Leith and Carver (all of the University of Wisconsin) and is called "The Foundations of National Prosperity."

There are also the "Saving Our Soils" Public Affairs pamphlets (bookstores $.10). Send to Washington for "To Hold This Soil," Miscellaneous Publication No. 321, by the United States Department of Agriculture. Stuart Chase well summarizes government awareness of the problem in "Rich Land, Poor Land." Katherine Glover does the same task in a popular form in "America Begins Again." Willson Whitman in 1939 wrote the story of the T.V.A. under the title of "God's Valley." A grand book is Archibald MacLeish's "Land of the

Free," with pictures tied together by poetic comment.

After a round of overwhelming statistics, consider the human consequences by looking into the Erskine Caldwell—Margaret Bourke-White "You Have Seen Their Faces." Steinbeck's "Grapes of Wrath" is a classic of migration from the pitiless "Dust Bowl." More comprehensively but less romantically the foundations of Steinbeck's thesis lie in Paul Sears' "Deserts on the March."

Index